# Shining the Light: Exposing the Truth

## The Coming New World Order

**Clayton Traylor**

PRESS

# Table of Contents

# Chapter 1

# The New World Order

"What is truth?" asked Pontius Pilate in John 18:38, while questioning Jesus before ordering his crucifixion. Throughout the history of mankind, there has been a war for our souls. Pontius Pilate would fit in with today's politicians well. He polled the crowd for their opinion. He did not believe in an objective truth, so he tried to pass the buck to Herod. Jesus and the Truth fared no better with Herod.

> "When Herod saw Jesus, he was greatly pleased, because for a long time he had been wanting to see him. From what he had heard about him, he hoped to see him perform a sign of some sort. He plied him with many questions, but Jesus gave him no answer. The chief priests and the teachers of the law were standing there, vehemently accusing him. Then Herod and his soldiers ridiculed and mocked him. Dressing him in an elegant robe, they sent him back to Pilate. That day Herod and Pilate became friends—before this they had been enemies. "
>
> *Luke 23:8-12*

Even though he could find no blame in Jesus, Pilate offered him up as a sacrifice. Today, our world leaders are very often weak willed and easily swayed by fear of public opinion, just as Pilate was. Others openly ridicule what is good and true, only being interested in what is right if there is some sort of payout for themselves.

The world leaders have handed down their values to the common man. Many today say they believe in right and wrong, but then when they are challenged, resort to a Machiavellian type of morality, where the ends justify the means. This can be seen in every bit of public life. Think about sports, where substance abuse is only frowned upon when the players get caught. In academics, students routinely pay others for their work, or access to old tests.

Society's moral degradation has become so widespread, though, that there doesn't have to necessarily be a reason behind an act. Less than a century ago, actors who lived openly in immorality, cheating on their spouses, and so on, were frowned upon by the public, and many people simply would not see movies that those people were in. The line, "Frankly, my dear, I don't give a damn," uttered by Rhett Butler in *Gone with the Wind* was shocking in 1939, and at least partly because profanity in films was rare, it became a memorable line. What film of today would have a line so tame be considered shocking and memorable?

In politics, we're used to having to choose "the lesser of two evils" because it's widely understood that the only type of politician is a corrupt one. On Wall Street, entities that are "too big to fail" are rewarded for corruption by bailouts. We're living in a world with people who have had their consciences "seared as with a hot iron" (I Tim 2:4) surrounding us at every turn.

These signs are frustrating to those of us trying to spread the Gospel throughout the world. This moral degradation and other signs that the end times are here are things that should be constantly on the mind of Christians today. We are exhorted in Romans 12:2 to "...not conform any longer to the pattern of this world, but be transformed by the renewing of your mind. Then you will be able to test and approve what God's will is – His good, pleasing and perfect will."

Postmodernist thought is rampant in our society. Postmodernism is a philosophical school of thought based specifically on the belief that there is no such thing as an objective truth, that everything is relative. This can be applied across any facet of human life, from arts and government, to science and religion. Nothing is sacred to the post-modernist, because it's all relative.

You would think, with a name like "Postmodernist," that this school of thought is something new, but it isn't. It has been in existence since the Garden of Eden, and their cause is picking up speed, fast. The serpent used the very same sort of logic to convince Eve to try the fruit of the Tree of Knowledge of Good and Evil. By taking the words of God and convincing her that they were only partly true, he convinced Eve that she would not be doing wrong by doing what felt good.

The Postmodernists have got many tricks at their disposal, and since truth is not something they feel bound by, they can easily, with no compunctions, take a sound bite or a passage from a book, and twist it to fit their own meaning. They take from the author the prerogative of using words with their own meaning so if you write a book, the Postmodernist will read it and deconstruct and reinterpret it to say whatever interpretation is most conducive to the goals of the hour. That meaning can even shift over time.

It's a movement against truth, meaning, and certainty, and is becoming the philosophy and mindset of the age. Men echo the sentiments of Pilate – there is no such thing as truth. We are told that you cannot find meaning in life, but paradoxically, you have to manufacture it yourself. Despite absolute uncertainty, we are told we can find true certainty within, providing that certainty falls in line with the approved agenda. We are so lost, certain that there is no meaning and no truth. It creates a vacuum, so that these powers are free to bring in that certainty with whatever "truth" suits them. We are told what to believe, and sadly, many of us follow without question.

Despite followers calling him Lucifer, which means "light bringer," Satan quite often operates in darkness. Post-modernism is a tool that is well suited to his tactics. Rather than having to deal with the fact that lies are rampant, the evildoers can simply circumvent that argument altogether with an appeal to subjectivism, and an "I'm okay; you're okay" mindset. Today, more than ever, there are tests to our faith, and this is one of the most pervasive. Christianity is a religion of peace, and many people can become confused with this deceptively peaceful sounding mentality appealing to our love for humanity.

You may have noticed that any common ground that a Christian might have had with which to build a rapport with non-believers has been rapidly disappearing in the last few decades. Values that were common to most Americans just 20 years ago are no longer held to. Our beliefs are being called a religion of hate, while we, Jesus' followers, are on the defensive on every side. We are scoffed at, ridiculed, and persecuted.

The world sees things differently than we do, and that is clear. However, some things aren't so clear. It's not just a moral degeneration we have to worry about, unfortunately. Although the struggle for good is being waged in the heart of every person alive today, there is a bigger, overarching coup taking place. If we are not aware of this larger, world scale war, then we will not be prepared for the assault coming at us, our families, and our country from without. We will be weakened.

There are currently groups on both sides of the political spectrum trying to fight corruption in government and the market, but have you noticed how even though the stated goals of groups can be virtually identical, they will quickly descend into bickering, slander, and malice? That's more of Satan's handiwork. Rather than being able to truly band together to protect our rights, we are distracted by the guiding hand of political pundits who sow strife and hatred. It is so easy to be caught up in it, but we've got to pull back and focus, rather than getting drawn into Satan's traps and being tools for evil.

The phrase "New World Order" is nothing new to us. We've heard it uttered by statesmen, presidents, and diplomats. We've even heard artists discussing the concept. In 1939, the popular novelist H.G. Wells said in his work, *The New World Order*, "Countless people will hate the new world order and will die protesting against it."

It's a familiar concept and a catchy phrase that many of us don't even notice any more, but what does it all mean? If we take the time to examine, alarming signs come to light. What are the goals of this movement, and what does God's word say about it? Chuck Missler, who is an author, evangelical Christian, Bible teacher, and the founder of the Koinonia House ministry, observed:

> I believe you and I are being plunged into a period of time about which the Bible says more than it does about any other period of time in human history - including the time that Jesus walked the shores of Galilee and climbed the mountains of Judea!

We have the tools to learn more about what is going on, and how to defend ourselves against this attack on our values and beliefs.

Simply put, the New World Order, after you peel back the beautiful phrasing and feel-good rhetoric, is a drive towards collectivism. Collectivism emphasizes interdependence, rather than independence, of all humans and governments. While that sounds similar to the structure of the early Christians on the surface, this is not a group of like-minded individuals working together for a common goal. This means *all* humans, and *all* governments, so that all people, no matter their beliefs and goals, will be subject to the whims and tyranny of the majority of the entire world.

Through a world government, it will be easier to enslave the human race, and strip us all of our God given liberties. Through a centralized religion, it will be easier to stamp out troublesome Christianity, complete with that inconvenient truth of John 14:6. There, Jesus tells us in very clear language that "I am the way and the truth and the life. No one comes to the Father except through me."

The powers that be have been planning a one world government for hundreds of years now, and that goal is becoming dangerously close to a reality. As a part of this one world government, there is also a movement towards a one world currency and a central religious institution setup to replace our traditional belief systems from the past is becoming more and more popular.

Though some of our leaders are simply weak-willed and available to the highest bidder, there are others who are able to control these pawns, steering them towards this goal. The United Nations, the Unitarian Movement, many peace accords and other world events have been pointing toward this goal all throughout the 20th and now 21st Centuries.

Secrets and lies are Satan's domain, and for years the powers of darkness have been moving, quietly, behind the scenes, to undermine the Truth. As long as we protect individual freedoms and the autonomy of individual governments, then there will be areas in which God's word can flourish, and there will continue to be havens for the Truth. Under the New World Order, there will be no such sanctuary. This so called "enlightened age" that we are being led into is a direct attack on God's people.

The trick is that this is all done under a guise of benevolence and helping out our fellow man. This is how the Lord of Lies works. A closer look reveals that cannot be the true agenda. If it were, why are misery and tyranny thriving in so much of the world, excused and condoned by governments who claim to oppose evil? Why is money being poured into causes that allow evil to thrive and good to be suppressed?

We need to take the time to give these movements a second look. The faithful of Christ must take note! We are given an easy way to test prophets in Matthew 7:15-20:

Watch out for false prophets. They come to you in sheep's clothing, but inwardly they are ferocious wolves. By their fruit you will recognize them. Do people pick grapes from thornbushes, or figs from thistles? Likewise, every good tree bears good fruit, but a bad tree bears bad fruit. A good tree cannot bear bad fruit, and a bad tree cannot bear good fruit. Every tree that does not bear good fruit is cut down and thrown into the fire. Thus, by their fruit you will recognize them.

What are the fruits of this move towards globalization of everything, from government, to currency, to even religion? As Solomon tells us in Ecclesiastes 1:9, "What has been will be again, what has been done will be done again; there is nothing new under the sun." That means that we can look at history to see God's reaction to man banding together for a one world government.

In Genesis 11, the men of earth banded together to "make a name for ourselves; otherwise we will be scattered over the face of the whole earth." This is the familiar history of the tower of Babel. This was another attempt of man to become all powerful and God-like, but this time everyone was banded together for the cause. What was God's reaction? It is evident that God did not want one world government. He "confused the language of the whole world" so that man could not achieve this self-serving aim. It stands to reason that His position has not changed, as man is just as sinful as ever.

Many Christians are not afraid to be thrown into prison because we realize we are free in Christ, no matter where we are, and that unbelievers are the slaves, and no matter where they are they are slaves to sin. However, this type of slavery isn't as simple as prison. It's not openly slavery. We can see, on a daily basis, more and more liberties being stripped from people in the name of safety or tolerance. While these are noble goals in and of themselves, we cannot allow them to cloud our judgment and keep us from digging deeper and truly examining what is going on all around us. But we are told, "It is for freedom that Christ has set us free. Stand firm, then, and do not let yourselves be burdened again by a yoke of slavery." (Galatians 5:1)

In order to do that, we must learn to follow the instruction to "stop judging by mere appearances, but instead judge correctly." (John 7:24) We can do that by reading and testing the words we hear on a daily basis to see if they are truth, or lies. Becoming intimately familiar with the scripture is imperative. That way, it will be readily apparent when we are being lied to.

The reason for this preparation is that these forces can have a beautiful appearance, one of peace-keeping and benign good will. The paths these forces lead us to will end in destruction, however. This front of good will and love is simply to make it appealing. It's far easier to be a fool than a wise man, but Proverbs has ample advice on how to become wise, and guard ourselves against the foolishness of the world. As long as we consult God's word regularly and properly, we have hope.

> For though we live in the world, we do not wage war as the world does. The weapons we fight with are not the weapons of the world. On the contrary, they have divine power to demolish strongholds. We demolish arguments and every pretension that sets itself up against the knowledge of God, and we take captive every thought to make it obedient to Christ.
>
> *2 Corinthians 10:3-6*

Remember the powerful prayer Jesus prayed for us:

> I have given them your word and the world has hated them, for they are not of the world any more than I am of the world. My prayer is not that you take them out of the world but that you protect them from the evil one. They are not of the world, even as I am not of it. Sanctify them by the truth; your word is truth. As you sent me into the world, I have sent them into the world. For them I sanctify myself, that they too may be truly sanctified.
> *John 17:14-19*

We are living in the world, however, even if we are not of it, and we must be aware of what is happening around us. Beyond God's word, we must keep current on world events, and watch for signs. These may be events that are mirrored in prophecy, or simply lies that become clear once they are tested. Take the information you find in this book and consider it carefully. Be watchful for evidence in daily life that points to the truth of what is going to be revealed in later chapters.

While many people are arguing about exactly when the end will come, it truly should not matter, because we are urged to be prepared always. In Matthew 25, Jesus tells the familiar parable of the ten virgins waiting for a wedding party. The party was long in coming, and all ten fell asleep. The bridegroom's arrival was announced, waking them all up. Half of these young women were unprepared, only bringing with them lamps, but no oil. They tried to borrow some from the five who had come prepared. Of course, there wasn't enough to spare, and so those five foolish virgins were left out in the dark.

While we do not know all of the future, we have God's word and prophecies to steer us. We should never believe that we don't need to prepare, or can depend on others to prepare for us. That way is foolishness. We must watch and be on guard at all times. Preparation is key, but so is observation.

In this day and age, we're dangerously close to another Babel scenario. The internet is making the world seem smaller than ever before. More and more people are able to communicate in a moment's time, across miles and continents, without even a delay of a second. We as humans are beginning to think of ourselves as all powerful, *if we only banded together under one government for the common good.*

William Cooper, who was an author, political activist, and radio show host until his death in 2001, warned us,

> . . . .the message that I am bringing to you is clear. It is concise, and there can be no mistake in its interpretation. You must wake up now or be enslaved. The war has begun many years ago. The war was declared by our enemies upon us. We are absolutely within our rights to restore our nation using any method or any manner that is required in so doing. You had better listen.

Throughout history, man has waged war, conquered and enslaved countless countries and men around the world. If you listen to secular history, the world seems to have no direction. It certainly can appear that there's a sense of accident about history and the cycle of world events. Historical figures such as Hitler, Mussolini, Mao, Stalin and many others seemingly rise to power in a political and philosophical vacuum. That is how our schools present these events. Is this true? Or is there a pattern laid with a planned direction? Is there a plan for the current direction of our world?

These are the things I hope to discuss in the coming book. It is my earnest goal in this work to wake up people to the perils we're facing. I want to reiterate William Cooper's thought to all of my readers. **You had better listen!**

There are plans, some of them Divine, and some evil. You must be ready. Make no mistake, this is no idle warning, and Christianity is under both direct and indirect attack. This shifting morality and the New World Order do threaten the freedom to worship, sometimes overtly, in the case of Communist China, and sometimes obliquely, through social stigma and worse. The goal of our enemy is the eradication of all that we believe in.

For the Christian, even worse than death, is the thought that our souls, or the souls of those we love, may be snared or led into a path that leads to spiritual death. Under the pretense of tolerance and love, there have been for centuries now, those who truly are corrupting our government, monetary systems, and most terrifyingly, our schools. Our faith is at stake, but so is the faith of our children, and our grandchildren.

Our nation was founded on principles that many are turning their backs on now. There are murmurings whenever the United States does not sign world-wide agreements. Take, for example, the Kyoto Accord. Using the leverage of loving the environment, advocates blatantly ignored the fact that it was clearly an attempt to target the United States while allowing other nations who are already far more guilty of destroying the environment to skate through with little responsibility. There are many other examples of this on the world stage. Our tax dollars are going overseas in charitable efforts that are seen by many as their due from the evil United States.

Glaring human rights violations are winked at in non-Christian nations, which would never be condoned in the United States. Obviously, the argument isn't that we should be allowed to commit atrocities, but the double standard that is placed on Christian nations is apparent.

Paul Warburg, who was on the Counsel of Foreign Relations and the architect of the Federal Reserve System, said in an address to the United States Senate, February 17, 1950, "We shall have World Government, whether or not we like it. The only question is whether World Government will be achieved by conquest or consent."

Those words are chilling, especially when the source is considered. This certainly implies that measures we take for granted now were put into place decades ago in achieving that goal. For the last century, prominent members of our government have clearly argued for a world government rather than our national sovereignty. If we place that sort of power in the hands of those who hate us, and cede our individuality as a nation, how will we be able to recover?

Further, how will we do God's work? Our mission is to go into all the world and teach the Gospel. If our religious and personal freedoms are subsumed by a world government, it will become more and more difficult to bring the news to all of humanity. If you have heard of the hardships and persecutions brought to our brethren overseas in nations that are antagonistic towards Christianity, then you can picture how that could spread.

# Chapter 2

He who sins is of the devil, for the devil has sinned from the beginning. For this purpose the Son of God was manifested, that He might destroy the works of the devil.
*1 John 3:8*

Jesus came to earth explicitly to destroy the works of the devil. Since we all have sinned, we all have been guilty of serving Satan ourselves. But as Christians now, we are fighting on Jesus' side. That means more than simply sinning no more. It means being prepared to also identify and destroy the works of Satan as we find them in our daily lives.

To understand the background, the purpose and history of this movement towards a New World Order, the first step is to understand the source. Satan has many names and mentions throughout the Bible and in the world today. He is slippery and hard to understand for many Christians, and ignoring our education on our enemy can be our most grave error.

It seems very evident in modern warfare – if we do not understand what the enemy is after, or what their arsenal consists of, how will we combat them? We will wander around in daily life, unaware until we are bombarded with a blindside attack. We have no chance of survival, much less conquering the enemy.

In spiritual warfare, the same principal applies. One tactic that is neglected by many Christians is this very crucial act of learning the nature of the enemy. To know the enemy is to be able to combat them. This means starting at the top learning about the figurehead and director of all opposition to the Lord's work on earth.

As we will discuss later, there are a surprising number of Satan's worshipers, or Luciferians, knowingly and purposely operating to bring about their agenda into the world. The Luciferian agendas are not always overt or easy to discern, but they are powerful and corrupting. Their traces can be seen in many political, religious, and monetary movements that affect our daily life.

Although some of the servants and proponents of this New World Order are knowingly in direct obedience to Satan's will, others are caught up in the momentum of a movement they truly do not understand. Whether they are willingly committing these crimes against Christ and God, or it is the result of the seeds that have been placed by others, or popular opinion, they are serving the wrong master.

In order that we do not make the same mistakes, we need to be intimately familiar with Satan's personality. It is naive to believe that if we go to church every week, and surround ourselves with people we trust, that we are truly preparing ourselves. Some people go a step further, and study their Bible – but tend to stay in a "comfort zone" where they do not challenge themselves or truly examine the Scriptures or what is going on in the world around them.

While that every day type of Christianity does make the average Christian feel very comfortable and safe, it is playing right into the hands of the New World Order. If knowledge of the enemy is put off, in our shielded environment we are blind to the issues affecting our lives. We are tricked into a type of complacency that can be deadly. Knowing the enemy can help us catch and thwart him far before he makes his "killing blows" to our freedoms.

Christianity might not be overtly named when our freedoms are attacked, but we must understand that it is one of the ultimate goals. Many of us have heard the quote from Pastor Martin Niemöller (1892–1984).

First they came for the
communists,
and I didn't speak out because I
wasn't a communist.

Then they came for the trade
unionists,
and I didn't speak out because I
wasn't a trade unionist.

Then they came for the Jews,
and I didn't speak out because I
wasn't a Jew.

Then they came for me
and there was no one left to speak
out for me.

Therefore, we must learn about our adversary, before it is too late. The Bible has a lot to say about Satan. By examining the passages that discuss him, we are given more information about his history, how he operates and what his aims are. Fully understanding his nature is fairly easy, just by taking a look at the different names and descriptors that are given throughout the scriptures to this enemy of God and man.

### *Satan the Fallen Angel*

In the beginning, before the world began, Satan was one of the Lord's angels, amongst his holy guardians. Jesus saw what we refer to as "the fall" - where Satan was evicted from heaven for his treachery and wickedness. Jesus says in Luke 10:18-20 that, "I saw Satan fall like lightning from heaven. I have given you authority to trample on snakes and scorpions and to overcome all the power of the enemy; nothing will harm you. However, do not rejoice that the spirits submit to you, but rejoice that your names are written in heaven."

Other passages discuss the fall of Satan, or Lucifer, in great detail. Isaiah 14 is an often quoted passage. Many newer versions completely cut out the term Lucifer, and instead use the translation "morning star" as is seen in the NIV version:

> How you have fallen from heaven,
>     morning star, son of the dawn!
> You have been cast down to the earth,
>     you who once laid low the nations!
> You said in your heart,
> "I will ascend to the heavens;
> I will raise my throne
>     above the stars of God;
> I will sit enthroned on the mount of assembly,
>     on the utmost heights of Mount Zaphon.
> I will ascend above the tops of the clouds;

I will make myself like the Most High."
But you are brought down to the realm of the dead,
    to the depths of the pit.

Those who see you stare at you,
    they ponder your fate:
"Is this the man who shook the earth
and made kingdoms tremble,
the man who made the world a wilderness,
    who overthrew its cities
    and would not let his captives go home?"
*Isaiah 14: 12-17*

Here, the ambitions of Lucifer are laid bare for us all to see. In his wickedness, he made the decision, "I will be like the most High." Later, we will find that Satan's appeal to Eve in the Garden of Eden is this same drive, the one that powers his own plans. There will be many gods under Satan's plan – he and all those who would follow him will be raised above the stars. This is a twisted version of the Lord's plan for us as Christians to partake in the Lord's glory. Often, Satan's plans have a grain of truth to them, but he takes that truth and corrupts it into something evil.

In the passage in Isaiah, the King James Version uses the word, "Lucifer." Since this is a hotly contested passage in Biblical hermeneutics, we should take a moment to address that. Since many would argue this passage refers to the King of Babylon alone, it would not make sense to discuss Satan in this light if there were no evidence to suggest it truly is the story of Satan's fall from heaven.

Note that there are plenty of passages throughout the Bible, particularly those prophetic in nature, that have dual purpose. They are what is known as a "double-reference principle", and there is an argument to be made looking at parallel passages in both the Old and New

Testaments that can shed further light on this passage, to see if in any part it is actually referring to Satan.

The first of these is Ezekiel 28. This passage tells a very similar story. The chapter addresses the king of Tyre and later the king of Sidon:

> The word of the LORD came to me:
> "Son of man, take up a lament concerning the king of
>   Tyre and say to him: 'This is what the Sovereign
>   LORD says:
> "'You were the seal of perfection,
> full of wisdom and perfect in beauty.
>   You were in Eden,
>   the garden of God;
> every precious stone adorned you:
>   carnelian, chrysolite and emerald,
>   topaz, onyx and jasper,
>   lapis lazuli, turquoise and beryl.
> Your settings and mountings were made of gold;
>   on the day you were created they were prepared.
> You were anointed as a guardian cherub,
>   for so I ordained you.
> You were on the holy mount of God;
>   you walked among the fiery stones.
> You were blameless in your ways
>   from the day you were created
>   till wickedness was found in you.
> Through your widespread trade
>   you were filled with violence,
>   and you sinned.
> So I drove you in disgrace from the mount of God,
>   and I expelled you, guardian cherub,
>   from among the fiery stones.
> Your heart became proud
>   on account of your beauty,
>   and you corrupted your wisdom
>   because of your splendor.

So I threw you to the earth;
    I made a spectacle of you before kings.
By your many sins and dishonest trade
    you have desecrated your sanctuaries.
So I made a fire come out from you,
    and it consumed you,
    and I reduced you to ashes on the ground
    in the sight of all who were watching.
All the nations who knew you
    are appalled at you;
    you have come to a horrible end
    and will be no more.'"
*Ezekiel 28:11-19*

While the king of Tyre was indeed evil, there are clues that this passage is also one with a double interpretation. To start with, there is no literal way that the king of Tyre that was being denounced in this passage was in Eden, or a "guardian cherub". This suggests that the author is referring not only to the literal human beings that were in this place of power, but also the power behind it, Satan himself.

The description of a fall of a mighty angel of great beauty fits this use as a literal interpretation. So while the king of Tyre is being called to task for his wickedness, and a fall from glory is predicted, the description of a glorious angel fallen and taken in depravity and sin to eventually be overthrown is also a well-accepted parallel interpretation of this passage.

Often New Testament passages help shed light on passages that the Jews of the time did not understand in their fullness. So it is logical that Jesus' reference to seeing the fall of Satan sheds light on these passages, as do other passages in Revelation, as well as others throughout the New Testament.

When we put these Scriptures together, we get a picture of an angel, who was with the Lord before the creation of the world. While we think of angels as beings of purity and goodness, they clearly have free will to choose their actions, because Satan chose to embrace violence and wickedness. His pride meant that he was no longer content with his station, and used these means to try and usurp the place of God.

> The great dragon was hurled down—that ancient
>     serpent called the devil, or Satan, who leads the whole
> world astray. He was hurled to the earth,
>     and his angels with him.
> Then I heard a loud voice in heaven say:
> "Now have come the salvation and the power
>     and the kingdom of our God,
>     and the authority of his Messiah.
> For the accuser of our brothers and sisters,
>     who accuses them before our God day and night,
>     has been hurled down."
> *Revelation 12:9-10*

Again, we get confirmation that Satan was thrown out of heaven. Satan, the Devil, and the serpent are all synonymous with the Dragon of Revelation. It is also clear that Satan was not alone in his plans or fall from grace.

He brought others with him when he fell, including other angels. If other angels can be corrupted, choosing the seductive wickedness of the Tempter, how much more dangerous is our position on earth? We are spiritual beings, but immersed in a physical reality that is far removed from the throne of God. What hope do we have? The next verse tells us that:

They triumphed over him
   by the blood of the Lamb
   and by the word of their testimony;
they did not love their lives so much
   as to shrink from death.
*Revelation 12:11*

Our Lord has shown repeatedly that he can even use evil to further his divine plan. The most obvious example of this is in the crucifixion of Jesus – God takes Satan's plans to thwart his Son on earth, and makes it an opportunity for the salvation of all of mankind. The blood of the Lamb, Jesus, is ours through this death.

Satan's wickedness is continually put to use, throughout all of history. In the prophecies that tells us what will become of the Dragon, we learn more.

### Satan as Tempter

The first time we encounter Satan in the Holy Bible is as the serpent in the Garden of Eden. In Genesis 3, we are told "the serpent was more crafty than any of the wild animals the LORD God had made..." and then we get to watch as he deceives Eve, and through her, Adam, out of the paradise God had prepared for them. Note in Genesis 3: 4-5, how he uses the truth and mingles it with a lie, "You will not certainly die," the serpent said to the woman. "For God knows that when you eat from it your eyes will be opened, and you will be like God, knowing good and evil."

This is typical of Satan. He twists the truth, making it difficult to decipher the truth from lies, because they are mixed in together. While hindsight may make it easy for us to see through his deception, in the moment the fruit will be like the fruit of the Tree of Knowledge of Good and Evil, "pleasing to the eye."

It is interesting that Luciferians throughout history continue to believe the original lie that the serpent told in the Garden of Eden that day. A strict look at the interpretation of the text shows that Eve was truly deceived, because her verb tenses do not agree with the Lord's when he informed her that on the day she partook of the fruit of the Tree of Knowledge, she would be sentenced to death. Also, it is important to note spiritual death came to Eve on that day.

However, Eve believed the serpent's lies and her own misunderstanding of the Lord's words. Today, having the same misunderstanding that Eve had, Luciferians will argue that the Lord was lying on that day. They believe that they will become as God, as long as they submit to the will of their chosen master. Unfortunately for them, their master is a liar and promises that which they cannot have.

In the book of Job, we get to see another direct attempt by Satan to subvert a human. Satan attends an assembly of the angels. (It is interesting that even though Satan has already fallen from his position, he still attends such assemblies.) Satan's discussion with God about Job shows a keen understanding of what motivates most men. His undermining and temptation of Job is painful to read, and most of us would fail such an extreme test as Satan puts Job through.

Satan tells the Lord that of course Job is faithful, because God has treated Job well. Satan immediately tries to whittle away Job's faith by taking away all that he has – both family and material possessions. When that doesn't work, he causes boils to cover Job's body, reasoning that even a man who is faithful will retreat in the face of physical pain.

When all of these fail, Satan's helpers come out. While we are not told they are in direct service to Satan, they certainly serve his ends. The first of these earthly servants of Satan turns out to be Job's own wife, who asks, "Are you still maintaining your integrity? Curse God and die!" (Job 2:9)

Job rebukes his wife, and does not sin. Then, Job gets a visit from his three closest friends. While maintaining a position of sympathy and advisory capacity, they try to get him to believe lies about the nature of God and himself. While they do not explicitly suggest he "curse God and die", they do sorely try his beliefs and provoke him. The warning is clear: Satan can often get help from well-meaning friends and loved ones.

Of course, perhaps the most famous failure of Satan's is his brazen attempt at corrupting the Son of God Himself. In Matthew 4, we are told that Jesus "was led by the Spirit into the wilderness to be tempted by the devil." (Matt 4:1) Jesus presents a much more formidable opponent to Satan's wiles than Eve did, and in the exchange we can see many of Satan's tactics.

First, in Matthew 4:3, Satan taunts Jesus. "If you are the Son of God, tell these stones to become bread." Satan can hone in on weakness, even that of Jesus' physical body suffering from the pangs of hunger and fatigue of fasting for 40 days in the wilderness. He also appeals to pride, and subtly suggests that if Jesus is God's Son, it's no big deal to use His power in any fashion. However, the very purpose of being led into the wilderness was to be tempted; Jesus cannot give in to the temptation.

After that attempt failed, Satan turns to twisting the truth, by quoting scripture to our Lord. This is a favorite tactic, taking that which is true and holy and perverting it, using it in a way that is contrary to God's will.

> Then the devil took him to the holy city and had him stand on the highest point of the temple. "If you are the Son of God," he said, "throw yourself down. For it is written:
>
> 'He will command his angels concerning you,
> and they will lift you up in their hands,
> so that you will not strike your foot against a stone.' "
> *Matthew 4:5*

Jesus, being well acquainted with the Scriptures himself, easily sidesteps this temptation with a passage more appropriate to the situation at hand, saying, "It is also written: 'Do not put the Lord your God to the test.' "

When all else seems to fail, Satan gives the same appeal to Jesus that he gave to Eve – promises of glory and power. Satan's great desire and ambition is to be worshiped above God.

> "Don't let anyone deceive you in any way, for that day will not come until the rebellion occurs and the man of lawlessness is revealed, the man doomed to destruction. He will oppose and will exalt himself over everything that is called God or is worshiped, so that he sets himself up in God's temple, proclaiming himself to be God."
> *2 Thessalonians 2:3-4*

To have God's very Son denounce all that he had for an earthly kingdom would have been the ultimate triumph. However, the flaw in Satan's temptation is that Jesus is God's Son. As such, he is unimpressed, and refuses to bow down and worship the devil. Satan then flees from him, true to James 4:7's admonition to "resist the devil, and he will flee from you."

### The Father of Lies

Jesus told his disciples that "My prayer is not that you take them out of the world but that you protect them from the evil one." (John 17:15) We know that this prayer applies to us, too, as his disciples. To be protected from the evil one, we must learn to love the truth. His biggest weapon is that of subverting the truth and telling lies.

Talking to the Jews who would eventually bring about his crucifixion, Jesus told them,

> "You belong to your father, the devil, and you want to carry out your father's desires. He was a murderer from the beginning, not holding to the truth, for there is no truth in him. When he lies, he speaks his native language, for he is a liar and the father of lies."
>
> *John 8:44*

When Jesus was brought to be tried for blasphemy and revolt against the Roman Empire, his enemies used lies to convict him. Not only that, they employed the force of politics and law, while not abiding by it themselves. A secret meeting of the Sanhedrin in the middle of the night was held on the fly. The accusers were not required to get a witness to corroborate the story.

When it became clear that even subverting Hebrew law was not going to be enough to deal with Jesus effectively, these enemies turned to Pilate and the state of Rome. Pilate did not want this burden, but when Pilate suggested they try him by their own laws, they admitted to their corrupt, twisted methods. They stated outright that they were using the laws of Rome to achieve what they could not in any other way. In John 18:31, we see they were turning Jesus over to Rome because "... we have no right to execute anyone."

Satan's technique for ruining men has not changed, and we are told it will not change, even until the day that the end of time comes. Throughout scripture we are warned that Satan is a deceiver who uses lies and the appearance of power and glory for his own goals. God will allow those who readily accept Satan's lies to have the free will to choose that path, even though it is one of lies.

> Don't let anyone deceive you in any way, for that day will not come until the rebellion occurs and the man of lawlessness is revealed, the man doomed to destruction. He will oppose and will exalt himself over everything that is called God or is worshiped, so that he sets himself up in God's temple, proclaiming himself to be God.

> Don't you remember that when I was with you I used to tell you these things? And now you know what is holding him back, so that he may be revealed at the proper time. For the secret power of lawlessness is already at work; but the one who now holds it back will continue to do so till he is taken out of the way. And then the lawless one will be revealed, whom the Lord Jesus will overthrow with the breath of his mouth and destroy by the splendor of his coming. The coming of the lawless one will be in accordance with how Satan works. He will use all sorts of displays of power through signs and wonders that serve the lie, and all the ways that wickedness deceives those who are perishing. They perish because they refused to love the truth and so be saved. For this reason God sends them a powerful delusion so that they will believe the lie and so that all will

be condemned who have not believed the truth but have delighted in wickedness.

*2 Thessalonians 2: 2-12*

These sorts of displays of power through signs and wonders serve the lie, and that wickedness deceives those who are perishing. They perish because they refused to love the truth and so be saved. For this reason God sends them a powerful delusion so that they will believe the lie and so that all will be condemned who have not believed the truth but have delighted in wickedness.

God forbid we be deceived by that powerful delusion! Let our eyes and hearts be open to the truth at all times.

Satan's wickedness is continually put to use, throughout all of history. In the prophecies that tell us what will become of the Dragon, we learn more. It is important to note that while Satan's status as an angel of heaven has been revoked, he is still called an angel throughout scripture. However, he still uses the guise to his own advantage.

The reality is that he is now, instead of the angel of light and goodness that he poses as, an angel of corruption and the Abyss. In Revelation 9:1, a scripture of prophecy and symbolism, we are told what John saw. "The fifth angel sounded his trumpet, and I saw a star that had fallen from the sky to the earth. The star was given the key to the shaft of the Abyss. "

In addition to usurping the glory and holiness that he could never attain in his wicked state, Satan similarly twists what is good and light to appear to be evil.

The Pharisees, who pitted themselves against Jesus during his ministry on earth, actually claimed that Jesus himself was serving Satan. This is one of many ironic passages about the Pharisees, and it tells us more of both

Satan's personality and the weaknesses of those who serve him accidentally. "But when the Pharisees heard this, they said, 'It is only by Beelzebul, the prince of demons, that this fellow drives out demons.' " (Matt. 12:24)

The Jews of Jesus' time were very aware of Satan, but these Pharisees were not able to recognize the son of God when they saw him. In part this is because Satan is such a deceiver, able to use the fact that they were too wrapped up in their own sense of holiness to see the truth. They served as Satan's ministers.

> And no marvel: for Satan himself is transformed into an angel of light. Therefore it is no great thing if his ministers also be transformed as the ministers of righteousness whose end shall be according to their works.
> *2 Cor. 11:14-15*

Even though they were aware of Satan's identity and on the lookout for him, they did not realize that it was their own goals that lined up with those of Satan. "What harmony is there between Christ and Belial? Or what does a believer have in common with an unbeliever?" the church at Corinth is asked in 2 Corinthians 6:15. Although the answer to this question is obvious to us, it eluded the Pharisees.

### We have been warned:

> "Don't let anyone deceive you in any way, for that day will not come until the rebellion occurs and the man of lawlessness is revealed, the man doomed to destruction. He will oppose and will exalt himself over everything that is called God or is worshiped, so that he sets himself up in God's temple, proclaiming himself to be God. "
> *2 Thess. 2:3,4*

Today in many realms, we can see man following along the same paths they have done since the beginning of time. Whether following in Eve's steps, and believing a twisted version of the truth, or becoming like those who were confounded at the tower of Babel, vaunting their own power above that of God, we can see this same progression happening.

### Satan in the End Times

Many people are deceived into thinking that Christianity is the evil religion. And this is exactly what Satan wants them to believe. Listen to 2 Corinthians 4:4 - "The god of this age has blinded the minds of unbelievers, so that they cannot see the light of the gospel that displays the glory of Christ, who is the image of God."

Even though Satan may be the "god of this age", he is a false god who is leading people astray from the true God. There will be a reckoning, and the Bible has much to say about how things will come about. While we will touch on this in greater detail in a later section, it would be neglectful to leave out the prophecies that have not yet come to pass about our Adversary.

Briefly, in Revelation, Satan is depicted by John as a star who falls out of heaven. He is given the keys to open up the Abyss. When he does so, a smoke rises out of the Abyss, and from that smoke a plague of locusts comes to earth to torture those who are unfaithful. Those who have the seal of God are not to be touched, nor are any plant or tree. This is the first woe told of in this cycle of the end times. Revelation 9:11 tells that these locusts "had as king over them the angel of the Abyss, whose name in Hebrew is Abaddon and in Greek is Apollyon (that is, Destroyer)."

The Destroyer will be granted, for a time, great power. This power will be of torment to those who are not amongst God's faithful. This show of power seems to show that Satan is indeed worthy of followers, and many have been and will continue to be led astray. However, those shows of power will be all for nothing, once Jesus comes again, and Satan's deceptions will ultimately be revealed, so that all will see the lies he has been telling.

Again, God puts the goals of his adversary to use in furthering his own goals in this struggle for the souls of humans. No matter what the Luciferians may believe about the superiority of their New World Order, or how it will be a reign of power for them, no matter what Satan may have promised, these people will not escape God's judgment. They will not like the inevitable end they meet:

> A third angel followed them and said in a loud voice: "If anyone worships the beast and its image and receives its mark on their forehead or on their hand, they, too, will drink the wine of God's fury, which has been poured full strength into the cup of his wrath. They will be tormented with burning sulfur in the presence of the holy angels and of the Lamb. And the smoke of their torment will rise for ever and ever. There will be no rest day or night for those who worship the beast and its image, or for anyone who receives the mark of its name." This calls for patient endurance on the part of the people of God who keep his commands and remain faithful to Jesus.
> *Revelation 14: 9-12*

Note the reminder in all of these verses. It is not only a caution to those who would follow Satan, but also an admonition to the faithful. We are told to love the truth.

We must be patient and endure. Over and over, we are cautioned that we must not fall into the trap of believing the lies of Satan. The reason is clear, that his quest for dominion is doomed for failure, and those who were on Satan's team will be dealt with accordingly.

But we have hope, as long as we are on guard, watchful and prayerful. The first step in this is to educate ourselves and be on guard. We must not forget who we are dealing with and must continue to look for Satan in not only the most obvious places, but also where we think it would be impossible to operate – right under our noses!

"Be alert and of sober mind. Your enemy the devil prowls around like a roaring lion looking for someone to devour." (1 Peter 5:8) Do not be caught off guard or devoured!

# Chapter 3

# Luciferianism

Now that we have discussed and looked into what the Bible has to teach us about our enemy, Satan, it's time to turn to look at his followers. Just like Christians, and all religions, Luciferians have many different belief systems and methods of operation. The end result is always the same, however. That is to undermine the work of the one true God, the God of Abraham, Isaac, and Jacob. The God we know and love as our Father and Creator.

William Cooper, the author and radio host, had this definition of Luciferianism in 1997:

> Very simply the Luciferian philosophy is, "Adam and Eve were held prisoner in the bonds of ignorance by an unjust and vindictive God in the Garden of Eden. They were set free from their chains (Evolution through "Primordial Knowing") by Lucifer (Prometheus) through his agent Satan in the guise of a serpent (ancient symbol of Wisdom) with the gift of Intellect (Fire). Through the use of his intellect man will perfect the race (Anglo/Aryan) and will himself become God (promise of Satan to Adam and Eve)." Any religion, church, organization, or People who believe they are

God, will become God, or are becoming God is practicing the Luciferian philosophy of the Mystery Schools, and are acting in furtherance of the conspiracy.

While the goal of this book is not to teach any of these philosophies, it will help significantly to understand who these people are, and what they believe. As you can see, there are many groups that fall under the Luciferian philosophy.

They venerate Lucifer, as described in various pagan texts and other writings, as a being represented by the planet Venus, or the morning star. The Holy Scriptures are actually included in the texts that are cited, since the word meaning "Lucifer" is also sometimes translated "Morning Star" and the meaning and entity are one and the same.

There are various sources for their teachings, some very, very old, showing us that Luciferianism has been practiced throughout mankind's history, and will continue to be a problem until the final battle. Sources such as ancient Egyptian, Roman and Greek mythologies are either borrowed heavily from or outright appropriated.

The early Christian offshoots of Gnosticism have plenty in common with Luciferianism. Western occultism today is also influential in the practices of those who knowingly practice Luciferianism, or even unknowingly are tainted by its teachings.

### Satanists

Some Luciferians identify as Satanists, while others would distance themselves from such an association. Either way, Luciferians often stress that Lucifer is the "light-bearer" aspect of Satan, trying to play up what they see as the positive angles of the Lucifer story as told in both the Bible and in other ancient writings.

However, there are some who take the name "Satanist" and own it proudly. These people as a group are rather diverse and resist categorization; however, we can broadly assign characteristics to different movements within them. The trend of Satanism began to really take hold in the 1960s, and grows stronger day by day. Generally, a Satanist sees the concept of "Satan" as a positive one, whether as a representation of a group of ideals, or as an actual personality.

There are Satanists who believe in Satan as a god or deity. These are called Theistic, or also Traditional, Satanists, by those of us who study them. They may believe in God as a "Prime Mover" - or creator God who was flawed and is out to get mankind. More often, however, they accept a "Deist" standpoint – there was a creation, but then that God let the world develop, or not, on its own, a totally hands off approach instead of the loving Creator and Father we know and love. They believe God plays no part in mortal lives whatsoever.

There are many subsets of Theistic Satanism. Some are polytheistic, with a strong belief in multiple gods, with Satan as one aspect of many choices that followers may affiliate with. There are many off-shoots and sister religions, like the Temple of Set, who worship other deities that are traditionally known to Christians as demonic in nature, and opposed by the Lord God.

These Theistic Satanists quite often do service and worship Satan, whether by ritual or just way of life. They have become more and more mainstream, pushing for religious protection and practicing openly. This is not something that is simply done in horror movies. This is happening in everyday life.

There are also those Satanists, known as Modern or Atheistic Satanists, who may be atheists altogether, agnostics, or simply not care whether a God (or gods) exists at all. Why would anyone be a Satanist if they didn't even believe in Satan? That's a puzzling concept, but it is rather as a concept that these Satanists choose to follow that path. Basically, they are holding to the belief system that has already been laid out by the Bible, which we have seen Satan to adhere to.

Both types of Satanists usually hold the self to be the central deity. That is, they worship themselves. Holding to the pattern from before the Garden of Eden, when Satan fell for his own arrogance from his privileged spot amongst the angels, Satanists are trying to become god-like. They want ultimate power for themselves. They want to do what they want to do, and that is the whole of their philosophy. Power by any means necessary, to serve themselves.

Another non-religious term for this point of view is ethical egoism. That is, the highest good a man can achieve is through acting in his own interest. The philosophy, whether centrally fixated on Satan or not, has become very pervasive in today's culture and we see its effects daily.

### Right Hand and Left Hand Paths

Many who are Luciferians deliberately practice magic. Some who study magic identify themselves as practicing "white magic" or "following the right hand path". These people are trying to advance themselves into deity status, worshipping themselves through pagan and occult ritual, but conforming to social mores and stigmas, and trying to be in harmony with society at large.

The Left Hand Path, on the other hand, tends to reject the notions of man-made or divine order or morality. In order to further self, these individuals throw off the constraints that society and ethics place on them and truly embrace their inner heathen, worshiping and fulfilling whatever wants and urges they have. As the famous artist Pablo Picasso once put it, "An artist must discover the way to convince his public of the full truth of his lies."

Usually those of the "Left Hand Path" who practice "black magic" distance themselves from this definition, saying both are simply means to the same end. For our purposes, knowing the differences between the two paths is interesting, but the warnings of those of the Left Hand Path are actually true. The problem is, those of the Right Hand Path seem more acceptable, and are much more likely to infiltrate our daily lives.

### The Religion of the Elite

Luciferianism has been the ruling class religion since the times of the ancient mystery and fertility religions. However, it has not disappeared at all. It continues, just as strong today as it ever was when there were temple prostitutes and seers in every city state in Greece. It is all based on the first lie that Satan sold to the world through deceiving Eve and then causing rebellion in Adam. That is, it is the lie that we all can become gods.

Lucifer is exalted in these mystery religions, as well as other societies that exist in the open in today's society, for example, Freemasonry, the Skull and Bones of Yale

University. There are even allegedly Christian religions that have been brought under suspicion of Luciferianism, such as the Jesuits and the Catholic Church.

Their influence is readily seen in almost every aspect of society. It is easy to see the spiritual blindness offered by Luciferian philosophy has blinded our world. When something takes on so many forms, we become numb and many do not even notice this happening. In reality, in Luciferianism, God the Heavenly Father, the redeemer of all born again believers, and His son, Jesus Christ, are vilified.

On the subject of Luciferianism, author and editor Phillip D. Collins states the following:

> Luciferianism is the product of religious engineering, which sociologist Williams Sims Bainbridge defines as "the conscious systematic, skilled creation of a new religion" (*New Religions, Science, and Secularization.*) In actuality, this is a tradition that even precedes Bainbridge. It has been the practice of Freemasonry for years. It was also the practice of Masonry's religions and philosophical progenitors, the ancient pagan Mystery cults."

> ...The inner doctrines of the Mesopotamian secret societies provided the theological foundations for the Christian and Judaic heresies, Kabbalism and Gnosticism. All modern Luciferian philosophy finds "scientific" legitimacy in the Gnostic myth of Darwinism. As evolutionary thought was popularized, variants of Luciferianism were popularized along with it... A historical corollary of this popularization has been the rise of several cults and mass movements, exemplified by the various mystical sects and gurus of the sixties counterculture The metastasis of Luciferian thinking continues to this very day."

If we go back to the beginning of time, we know that there were two sources of truth. First, there was the Tree of the Knowledge of Good and Evil, and there was the Tree of Life in the garden. The Tree of the Knowledge of Good and Evil holds the knowledge of what is right and wrong; it's the letter of the law of God and the dead religion based on compliance to the dead letter of the law. It is man-made compliance to law, and man-made changes in outward behavior.

Luciferianism holds that the serpent, whether Satan's servant or his own physical manifestation, brought humans the Light – that is the knowledge that the Tree of Knowledge held. Other ancient religions have corollaries to this positive spin on the creation tale. For example, there is the story of Prometheus, giving man fire (light) as a gift, freeing mankind from his place amongst the animals (or in the Garden of Eden).

However, this knowledge is a focus on self. If we focus on ourselves, we can go two directions: we can indulge and become licentious and hedonistic. This is easily seen as evil to most people, even those who are not Christians. It is why those following the so-called "Left Hand Path" or who are blatant Satanists do not make nearly as much headway in corrupting the world.

Sadly, we can go another route, which is a problem with some churches: we can become self-righteous. Still, there is the focus on self, which is hypocrisy. On this very matter, Jesus said, in Matthew 6:2, "So when you give to the needy, do not announce it with trumpets, as the hypocrites do in the synagogues and on the streets, to be honored by men. I tell you the truth, they have received their reward in full."

These hypocrites have a false trust that worldly philosophies and other fruit of the tree of knowledge of good and evil will expose Satan. However, it will not, because, we must always remember that Satan appears as an angel of light.

Remember how much we have placed in the basket as it was passed around at church? Well, Satan was willing to give Christ the entire world on that mountaintop. How's that for a donation? How many people think they can buy their way into heaven, whether with donations or "good deeds" all done for show? It's egoism, the philosophical twin to Luciferianism.

"For everything in the world—the cravings of sinful man, the lust of his eyes and the boasting of what he has and does—comes not from the Father but from the world." (1 John 2:16) The fruit of the tree of knowledge will not expose Satan, because it appeals to the lust of the eyes, the flesh, and the pride of life. That knowledge leads to spiritual and physical death in both the Garden of Eden, and in our lives today. That searching for godhood also produces lasciviousness, double mindedness, and pride in what one knows. The goodness of man is a popular concept.

There was another type of knowledge that came from the tree, however, and that is the knowledge of good. This includes the fear of God, Peace, and God-centered knowledge (that is, relevant to what God's plans and purpose are,) and wisdom. It brings the spirit of the law and a living faith and relationship with Yahweh, our God. That spirit, in turn, changes the heart of the believer, bringing a focus on Christ, the Holy Spirit and the Heavenly Father.

To expose Satan and his influences, we must continually be using the living word of God written with the guidance of the Spirit. Instead of a fleshly focus, it is a spiritual focus. This leads to life, not to mention a renewed sound mind and humility to learn from the others and from the master teacher. It preaches the goodness of God. Of course, "the man without the Spirit does not accept the things that come from the Spirit of God, for they are foolishness to him, and he cannot understand them, because they are spiritually discerned." (I Cor. 2:14)

In the Bible, and in church, you often hear about the fall of man, the Genesis story of Eve being tempted by the serpent. In the mystery schools of the Luciferians, however, this mystical power (fleshly knowledge) coming out of the age of innocence (in the Garden of Eden) is the Luciferian philosophy. They've tried to illuminate you with this for years from a radio broadcast. These two stories are the same tale, told from vastly different points of view. There's only one difference between the Luciferian philosophy and the fall of man, and that is those who talk about the fall of man believe in God, whether or not they believe in a Savior. They believe in the God of the Old Testament, the Great I AM.

The ones who believe in the Luciferian philosophy do not truly believe in God or His Word. General Albert Pike, a Freemason and Civil War general who was steeped in these traditions, writing in *Morals and Dogma*, explains it this way:

> Illuminism is really the religion of a benevolent mythical Lucifer-not Satan. It is disguised as political idealism, bent on eradicating religion and monarchies in general, and Christianity in particular, and gaining global control for a "commonwealth of nations" featuring "universal democracy."

He used the gnostic name for the God of the Bible, *Yaldaboath*. This is a term that the Gnostics called the demiurge. The Gnostic tradition, in the early church, came from a corruption of Christianity. This was an early pairing of the Greco-Roman mystery religions, Zorastrianism, Hellenistic polytheism, and other sects. The roots of Luciferianism were strong, even in the early days of the church. The story is that this demiurge, "Father of Chaos" was an inferior god, despite being the creator of the world.

This concept has been seen as a metaphor for religion in general, and some Luciferians see the story this way – Yaldaboath is human created, so therefore he is bound by human limits and imagination. Humans want to know God, but our own limitations keep us from experiencing divinity, in our own forms. See again the emphasis on self, on rising above and becoming divine, of using intellect to sublimate the human condition to godhood.

Albert Pike paints the picture of God, not as the benevolent Father we know, but this lesser god, who created Adam and Eve and the world. This demiurge, or Yaldaboath, created them flawed and then abandoned them in the age of innocence. Then Pike describes devils who allegedly forbade Adam and Eve to eat from the Tree of Knowledge of Good and Evil. Lucifer sends his agent, Satan, who is seen as an angel of light. This is the serpent, who gives them permission to eat of the tree.

> "...Among Luciferians (sic), god is seen as evil, trying to keep knowledge away from man. The same scenario was repeated in the Garden of Eden, when the snake explained to Adam and Eve that God didn't want them to have knowledge that would make them wise."

Adam and Eve, previously held prisoner in the Garden of Eden, were set free by the gift of intellect. Through the use of this intellect, man will receive redemption and conquer the earth and nature. He will become as the other gods. Pike further notes that "to the secret societies, Lucifer is always depicted as a benevolent, peace-loving god with nothing but the best intentions for the human race." These secret societies included the Freemasons that Pike himself was a part of, so he would have first hand knowledge.

General Albert Pike, interestingly, is one of two Freemasons who have the honor of being buried in the house of the temple in Washington D.C. He held the office of "Sovereign Grand Commander of the Council, Grand Sovereign's Council of the 33$^{rd}$ degree". This may have been the highest office of Freemasonry in the United States at that time.

General Pike claims to be an Anti-Christ and a Luciferian. He mocks Christianity and denies the virgin birth and the resurrection of Jesus Christ. He even calls the early Christian fathers, "dunces." In his book *Morals and Dogma*, Albert Pike sings the praises of Lucifer:

> "Lucifer, the Light-bearer! Strange and mysterious name to give to the Spirit of Darkness! Lucifer, the Son of the Morning! Is it he who bears the Light, and with its splendors intolerable, blinds feeble, sensual, or selfish souls? Doubt it not!"

He objects to the portrayal of the malignant nature of the Satan as depicted by Christians:

> "The true name of Satan, the Kabalists say, is that of Yahveh reversed; for Satan is not a black God, but the negation of

God. The Devil is the personification of Atheism or Idolatry. For the Initiates, this is not a person, but a force, created for good, but which may serve for evil. It is the instrument of Liberty or free will. They represent this Force, which presides over the physical generation, under the mythologic and horned form of the God Pan; thence the he-goat of the Sabbat, brother of the Ancient Serpent, and the light bearer or Phosphor, of which the poets have made the false Lucifer of the legend."

This story is taught in every Masonic Temple. There were instructions left that leave no question as to Albert Pike's seriousness. On July 14, 1889, to the 23 Supreme Councils of the world in *La Femme et l' Enfant dans la Franc-Maconnerie Universelle,* it records these instructions:

"That which we must say to the crowd is – We worship a God, but it is the God that one adores without superstition.

"To you, Sovereign Grand Inspectors General, we say this, that you may repeat it to the Brethren of the 32nd, 31st and 30th degrees – The Masonic religion should be, by all of us initiates of the high degrees, maintained in the purity of the Luciferian doctrine.

"If Lucifer were not God, would Adonay (The God of the Christians) whose deeds prove his cruelty, perfidy, and hatred of man, barbarism and repulsion for science, would Adonay and his priests, calumniate him?

"Yes, Lucifer is God, and unfortunately Adonay is also God. For the eternal law is that there is no light without shade, no beauty without ugliness, no white without black, for the absolute can only exist as two Gods : darkness being necessary to light to serve as its foil as the pedestal is necessary to the statue, and the brake to the locomotive.

"In analogical and universal dynamics one can only lean on that which will resist. Thus the universe is balanced by two forces which maintain its equilibrium: the force of attraction and that of repulsion. These two forces exist in physics, philosophy and religion. And the scientific reality of the divine dualism is demonstrated by the phenomena of polarity and by the universal law of sympathies and antipathies. That is why the intelligent disciples of Zoroaster, as well as after them, the Gnostics, the Manicheans and the Templars have admitted, as the only logical metaphysical conception, the system of the two divine principles fighting eternally, and one cannot believe the one inferior in power to the other.

"Thus, the doctrine of Satanism is a heresy; and the true and pure philosophic religion is the belief in Lucifer, the equal of Adonay; but Lucifer, God of Light and God of Good, is struggling for humanity against Adonay, the God of Darkness and Evil."

Note all of the references, to Gnostics, Templars, Zoroastrianism, and so on. These are not just names dropped in the middle of a speech. There are secret brotherhoods, societies, mystical temples, and occult organizations, not just in this land but the world over, teaching this Luciferian philosophy. Albert Pike is just one of many. These are outright statements of belief that God is evil, and Lucifer is goodness and light.

The Luciferian philosophy has been seen in some of the most influential people from the last few hundred years, for example, Karl Marx, the father of so many revolutions and one of the most influential people of the 19th century. Many believe Marx to be an atheist. The following excerpts certainly leave that up to debate.

Marx in a poem called *The Player*, later down-played by both himself and his followers:

The hellish vapors rise and fill the brain,
Till I go mad and my heart is utterly changed.
See this sword? The prince of darkness sold it to me.
For me beats the time and gives the signs.
Ever more boldly I play the dance of death.

In his poem *The Pale Maiden*, Marx writes:

Thus heaven I've forfeited, I know it full well.
My soul, once true to God, is chosen for hell.

And one last Marx poetry quote:

Then I will be able to walk triumphantly.
Like a god, through the ruins of their kingdom
Every word of mine is fire and action.
My breast is equal to that of the creator.

These are not the words of simply an atheist. Even if that argument were to be made, the end result would be the same. Marx saw a different path, the path of Lucifer, and decided to take it. He wanted to become "equal" to God.

Another example is Manly B. Hall, a leading occult philosopher and Mason of the 33rd degree, who taught throughout the twentieth century. He stated in his work *The Lost Keys of Freemasonry,*

"When the Mason learns that the key to the warrior on the block is the proper application of the dynamo of living power, he has learned the mystery of his craft. The seething energies of Lucifer are in his hands and before he may step onwards and upwards he must prove his ability to properly apply (this) energy."

Now, an assertion that these influential people and world leaders are in control of the world as slaves of Lucifer may seem far-fetched, but it's based on some of the actual writings of the elite themselves. There have even been observed rituals. One of the most famous cases of this is when filmmaker and broadcaster Alex Jones filmed from inside the Bohemian Grove. The grove is a retreat where every year, some of the most influential people in the United States and around the world, including heads of state and royalty, come together.

Alex Jones recorded an event where the establishment's elite, the ones who rule the world, travel to this Bohemian Grove. This grove is in Sonoma County in northern California, a 2700 acre grove of redwoods. These world elite are meeting there to indulge in their obsession with the occult. These meetings are purported to include everyone from presidents and prime ministers, governors, heads of banking and industry, academics, media, and many other celebrities from Hollywood. Only 2000 or so make the cut to be the privileged few who meet together to engage in bizarre, ancient, Canaanite Luciferian, Babylonian mystical religion ceremonies!

A quote from the Alex Jones show, about the particulars of the Grove:

> "Membership in the Grove is by invitation only and its membership is determined by such factors as social standing, occupation, and personal connections. Privacy is one of the grove's most cherished virtues. Members may not photograph, record, speak or write about activities at the retreat. While many public officials are Grove members, the press are a distinctly unwelcome guest."

Over and over, we can see what is done in secret, has come out into the world. This is not just a matter of a difference in theological opinion. This is purely hatred against the God of the Bible. This extends outward to hatred against our Lord Jesus Christ, and even to Christians and Christian society. That is truly what is meant in this religion and philosophy.

### In Revelation, John, from the Isle of Patmos, writes,

> Then I saw the beast and the kings of the earth and their armies gathered together to make war against the rider on the horse and his army. But the beast was captured, and with him the false prophet who had performed the miraculous signs on his behalf. With these signs he had deluded those who had received the mark of the beast and worshiped his image. The two of them were thrown alive into the fiery lake of burning sulfur. The rest of them were killed with the sword that came out of the mouth of the rider on the horse, and all the birds gorged themselves on their flesh.
>
> *Revelation 19: 19-21*

It is easy to think that the kings of the earth and their armies probably do not like fighting, and further, do not realize what they truly are doing. But more and more study of these secret societies and religions leads to a conclusion that perhaps they know exactly what they are doing. Maybe not all, especially the blind followers, and many Masons may not realize what they are doing. However, it is clear from writings from today and centuries past, that many of these men, especially the leaders, know exactly what they are doing. They are aware that they are waging war against the Lord God, and they reject all he stands for. They believe him to be a being of evil and weakness.

Where did these people get their ideas from? Obviously, the source is Satan. Next, however, we need to take a trip through the last couple of centuries of history, to discuss some key players in forwarding the agenda of Lucifer.

## Chapter 4

# Theosophy and Helena Blavatsky

W hile the roots of Luciferian philosophy are ancient as Satan himself, there are prominent personalities in the past few centuries that really brought it to legitimacy in mainstream thought. One of these was Madame Helena Blavatsky. She claimed to bring forth ancient knowledge to the west, to illuminate the darkness of Christianity as it was in Europe and America at that time. From the roots of the movement that she founded, we can trace many of the most powerful Luciferians and proponents of the New World Order. Her story and beliefs are vital to understanding the movement today.

### *Freemasonry and Occultism*

Madame Blavatsky was born Helena Petrovna von Hahn on July 31, 1831, to a noble Russian family. She was named after her mother, Helena Andreevna von Hahn, a notable female novelist. The subjects of her mother's writings were, not surprisingly, feminist in nature in a time and place where women did not generally do much writing or venturing into the intellectual realm.

Young Helena was schooled at home, spending much time in her grandparents' library. There was an extensive section on the occult, and this topic especially ignited the imagination of the young girl. She claimed to hear voices and observe phenomena with such ardency and vehemence that many believed that these were no mere fairy tales of a young child, but actual accounts of visitations and clairvoyance.

Helena's grandfather also had many books on Freemasonry. Freemasonry has its roots shrouded in mystery, but we do know that as late as the 16th and 17th centuries it had become more and more prevalent. These secret societies were well known but little understood at the time, as is still true today. These topics dovetailed neatly with the occultic and esoteric interests that Helena was cultivating.

She married at the age of 18, but that marriage quickly proved to be a sham. She was no longer considered a child by virtue of this marriage, and when she returned to her family for a while, she quickly asserted her independence and began a series of travels that would take her around the world at least three times over.

### Continuing Education

Helena Blavatsky's travels led her all over the world, on the orders of some mysterious "Teacher" that she refers to in her writings. She believed that her work would pave the way to the freedom of the human mind, and that she must travel far and wide to discover universal truths to all religions and belief systems. She took part in séances and spoke to spirits regularly. She was well known in spiritual circles the world over, and many people competed to have her sit in and discuss the occult with them, or else to take part in their rituals.

Whether her "teacher" truly existed or not, is unclear. She may have simply been a charlatan, preying on the gullibility of those around her, or she may have actually had some sort of demonic mentor. There are many undocumented accusations, for example that she smoked marijuana, and was a spy for the Russians or the English. Her wide travels lead to a great deal of conjecture, and her own recounting of the time is jumbled and distorted, so that the truth of a time line and what actually occurred is hard to determine.

Helena Blavatsky spent extensive time in India and other parts of Asia, learning the culture and religions there. She repeatedly tried to enter Tibet, finally succeeding, to learn the ancient "truths" that would be revealed to her there. She also said that she needed to spend some time in quiet meditation, preparing her for the life purpose she believed was set before her. She even claimed to have been a soldier, fighting alongside Giuseppe Garibaldi, even though such claims were impossible to substantiate.

What is not hard to determine, however, is what she actually accomplished once she began to write and combine her efforts with others. Here there is a trail and a record of what she said and did that we can observe. She was a prolific writer who gained a great following, and to this day influences many people the world over. It is very likely that some of the beliefs you hold, as a part of western culture, actually began with her words.

We can really start to trace her steps definitively in about 1874. It was then that during one of her travels to the United States, she met Henry Steel Olcott. This man, widely known as the first American Buddhist, was currently studying and writing a series at that time for séances that were being held in Chittenden, Vermont. These séances at the Eddy brothers' farm were a natural draw for someone like Helena, whose claims of clairvoyance continued throughout her life. Eventually, these two, together with a third, William Quan Judge, formed the cornerstone of the first Theosophical Society.

This quest for knowledge is mirrored and mimicked over and over by the New Age movement, over a century later. Often people will go out in search of spiritual enlightenment and knowledge, and they travel to Asia, Tibet and India in particular, to learn of the masters. In fact, the adherents of Theosophy today claim that the Tibetan masters have an ancient knowledge that they periodically send a messenger out into the world at large to teach.

### Theosophy

What was this message that Helena Blavatsky was commissioned with? The word itself means "knowledge of the Divine," but that knowledge isn't about Jehovah. Theosophy comes in a very attractive package. Similarly to the Dalai Lama himself, the Tibetan message that Helena Blavatsky taught had a heavy focus on compassion, and in fact the woman did perform some very compassionate works. As we delve further into the teachings, we can divide them up into a few tenets.

Blavatsky, in her writings, retells the history of the world, from the creation to the present. She draws from her travels and learnings of occult and religions throughout the world, combining Babylonian astrology,

Egyptian hieroglyphics, the Hindu and Buddhist religions, and the popular spiritualism. Her works made her a best-selling author and one of the most influential people that have come from Russia, ever.

The Theosophical Society that she helped to form had as a stated aim, the pursuit of a universal brotherhood of humanity without man made differences, such as color, class, creed, or beliefs. The one belief that had to be held was in this very brotherhood, and furthering the goal of attaining it. They were out to study comparative religion, as Helena had already done throughout her travels, trying to unite all of the world's religions into one common thread.

Studies of science, philosophy, and the unexplained – whether the power of man or that of nature – were also part of the goals of the society. All of this fits in nicely with a goal of uniting the world under a universal brotherhood. It sounds rather benign and even all inclusive, compassion and finding the common in all men, doesn't it? Remember, though, that Satan appears as an angel of light.

Early on, Blavatsky set out to correct what she saw as the superstitions that had arisen in religions, including Christianity. She accused the church of going out of its way to twist the words of the Bible and misrepresent Lucifer as our enemy, calling him wrongly "Satan", or "enemy", in order to further the dogma of the time. For example, she quotes Dr. A. Kingsford's book "Perfect Way" (section "The Secret of Satan"): "It is Satan who is the god of our planet and the only god" and adds "and this without any allusive metaphor to its wickedness and depravity."

Not only in her quoting and defense of others, but in her own writings, her beliefs are clearly laid out. In her many works, it becomes clear that Blavatsky was very much a Luciferian, utterly deceived and smitten by that powerful, benevolent image that Satan put forward falsely. She stated in her work, the *Secret Doctrine: Volume I, Cosmogenesis:*

> "The devil is now called Darkness by the Church, whereas, in the Bible he is called the 'Son of God' (see Job), the bright star of early morning, Lucifer (see Isaiah). There is a whole philosophy of dogmatic craft in the reason why the first Archangel, who sprang from the depths of Chaos, was called Lux (Lucifer), the 'Luminous Son of the Morning,' or manvantaric Dawn.

Manvantara is Hindu time cycle, based on their cosmology. See how easily she combines religions? Madame Blavatsky is one of the original purveyors of the idea that all paths can lead to the same end. However, we know better than to conflate any other paths with that of the one true path, Christianity.

In *The Secret Doctrine, Volume II, Anthropogenesis,* Blavatsky even flatly states that Satan is a Savior figure.

> In this case it is but natural – even from the dead letter standpoint – to view *Satan*, the Serpent of Genesis, as the real creator and benefactor, the Father of Spiritual mankind. For it is he who was the 'Harbinger of Light,' bright radiant Lucifer, who opened the eyes of the automaton *created* by Jehovah, as alleged; and he who was the first to whisper: 'in the day ye eat thereof ye shall be as Elohim, knowing good and evil' – can only be regarded in the light of a Saviour.

Many would cite her correct conjectures in the field of science, regarding the nature of the atom and the like, to try and soften this belief system. But, no matter how appealing the packaging, or how right she may have been in worldly matters, this is Luciferianism. There is no disguise even attempted.

To further put to rest any ambiguity, there is also a struggle to become divine that is laid out for the adherent of Theosophy. Blavatsky describes that she is one in a series of "Hidden Masters". The Theosophical Society is one of many attempts by these masters to guide humanity into an overall Intelligent Cosmic Evolutionary scheme. This would be the evolution of mankind towards the ultimate goal: the attainment of perfection. This hierarchy is a mirror of the hierarchy of the Freemasons that influenced her so much in earlier life.

### Nazism

One person who was greatly influenced by Helena Blavatsky's writings was none other than the man that many of us cite as the absolute embodiment of evil in the last century. Adolf Hitler was a great fan of her writings, and reportedly read from her works on a daily basis. He was reported to have slept with a copy of her book, *A Secret Doctrine* by his bedside.

The Swastika was a major symbol of the Theosophical Society, whose seal included it, as well as the Star of David, for Christianity and Judaism. The Ankh represented the key of life and was part of the ancient Nile religions. The Om symbol, one that we are increasingly familiar with in our own culture, a Hindu meditative symbol, and the Ouroboros symbol were also a part of the seal. Ouroboros, interestingly, is a serpent eating its own tail.

The reason that Hitler focused on the swastika, however, is that he was enamored of some of the racial views that Blavatsky presented. She was one of the first

Westerners to use the term Aryan, and the Swastika was supposed to be the symbol of the Aryan race. She believed in five races, and the Aryan one was the current supplanter and world dominant culture. She denounced the Semite races as "degenerate in spirituality and perfected in materiality."

Is it any wonder that someone as power-hungry as Adolph Hitler would be lured by the promise of godhood that Satan offers? In the 1935 Nazi propaganda film, *Triumph of the Will* - the very name reflects these ideas – Hitler can be heard saying, "It is our wish and will that this State and this Reich last for thousand years. We can be happy to know that this future belongs entirely to us!"

The influences that shaped this man's world, and consequently, the rest of the world and history of the Twentieth century, cannot be swept under the rug, no matter how much Theosophical disciples try to distance themselves from the man and the atrocities he committed. They can argue that Helena Blavatsky was all for compassion and understanding. His racial programs may have been a misunderstanding and distortion of the way she presented the five races of mankind. But it was her emphasis on the occult, the power of the self-made god, and these ancient mysteries that called to Hitler.

In the 1930s, there was a time that made the rise of Hitler's Nazi party possible. During this period, Germany had become fascinated, as a nation, with the occult. And this interest was exactly what Hitler needed to draw on for his audiences.

Denis de Rougemont, the Swiss author and non-conformist, had listened to one of Hitler's famous speeches and observed the reaction of the crowd to his charisma.

He noted that he seemed to have a supernatural effect on the audience:

> 'Some people think, from having experienced in his presence a feeling of horror and an impression of some supernatural power that he is at the seat of Thrones, Dominiations and Powers", by which St. Paul meant those secondary spirits which can descend into any ordinary man and occupying him like a garrison.
>
> I have heard him pronounce one of his great speeches. Where do the superhuman powers he shows on these occasions come from? [...?]
>
> He was fundamentally an insignificant little man with strong patriotic feelings and a passion for social reforms. He functioned on a low-level and there were limits to his dreams.
>
> Suddenly, as if by miracle, he surged to the front and was successful in everything he undertook. But the medium who is possessed by outside forces is not necessarily conscious of their strength nor of the direction in which they are leading him.
>
> He dances to a tune which is not his own. Until 1934 he thought he was doing all the correct steps. But he was not keeping strict time.
>
> He thought that all he had to do was to make full use of his ' and Powers'.
>
> But one cannot use such Powers; one can only serve them.

This is true of Satan. Many of the Luciferians are deceived into believing they can wield these types of powers for their own goals, which they may believe to be for the good of mankind. But in reality, they are only serving the enemy of all mankind.

## *A Major Influence on Western Culture Today*

Freemasonry is an esoteric version of Luciferian beliefs, made for an elite group to hold their meetings in secret, with plans for all of us. On the other hand, whether she was truly taught by some mystical teacher or not, Helena Blavatsky is directly responsible for spreading these ideas to a broader base, and bringing them into the mainstream of western culture.

These influences take many forms. Many of us view the New Age movement as harmless feel-good rhetoric, but is that true? Is there really a more sinister agenda being promoted?

Remember, Hitler completely changed the face of the world in the last century, and he took many of his beliefs directly from Theosophy. There are other largely influential people that took up the banner, and as the movement evolved, its strength grew. We can't underestimate the power of these messages.

Hinduism is currently undergoing a surge in popularity, begun in the 1960s by celebrities, but having its roots in the beliefs of this one Russian expatriate, writing from her adopted home in London in the last decade of the 19th Century. That, blended with psychology that is often as self-improvement, self-hypnosis, positive thinking and self-help culture has weakened our resolve. How many have listened to Oprah talk about "the Secret" or other visualization techniques? It's quite possible that today's world is in much more danger than even the Nazi Germany that adored Adolf Hitler.

"But, surely we're not as corruptible as all that!" we think, as we go to church and participate in clearly Christian behaviors. But, as we will explore later on, there is a trend in our thinking to make us more receptive to these types of influences. We will continue to see how that influence has grown to become a frighteningly large part of our daily reality.

# Chapter 5

# Prominent Disciples of Blavatsky

Madame Helena Blavatsky was not the only person of note that brought this brand of Luciferianism to the forefront in the 19th Century, but she was a great influence. Her disciples continued to embrace New Age concepts, particularly those of the ascended masters and the understanding of Lucifer, the light-bringer. They proselytized far and wide, persuading more and more people to come under their spell.

Names you have heard before, often in the Self-Help section of the library, or the Spiritual/New Age section, such as Edgar Cayce, Benjamin Creme, and Napoleon Hill, were, if not outright Theosophists or disciples of Blavatsky's teachings, certainly influenced heavily by them.

Often these prominent names, whose works have stood up throughout the past century, also were Freemasons, whether secretly or openly. The Freemasons are widely considered to be amongst the most charitable, benevolent societies in the world. They do not allow admittance if you do not believe in a higher being. Their secrecy protects them from outside scrutiny that would really reveal the truth. The irony is, that with their occult rituals emphasizing the ascendency of mankind, and the Luciferian belief system they are taught, that status is very questionable. Are they simply another group of Satan's workers, disguising themselves as angels of light?

Amongst the most notable of these people who followed in Helena P. Blavatsky's wake, was Alice P. Bailey, who, together with her husband, Foster Bailey, went on to set up the widely respected and ever powerful Lucis Trust. Another dramatic example is the preeminent Manly P. Hall, whose teachings many have traveled far and wide to study, paying great sums of money to learn the secrets of the ancients that he promised his audiences.

### Alice Bailey and Lucis Trust

Alice Bailey was born in England in 1880, and moved to the United States in 1908, so she came along right after Helena Blavatsky's time. She grew up in a conservative English family with a purported strong faith in Christ and the Lord. She even did missionary work in India with the YMCA and the British army. In her own words, about the writing of her autobiography, she said, "It might be useful to know how a rabid orthodox Christian worker could become a well-known occult teacher."

The story is told that her husband was purportedly not the ideal Christian husband, and after claims of abuse, she left her marriage with her three children. The feelings of resentment and mistreatment that she felt towards her husband carried over into Christianity, and she left the faith as well.

Alice Bailey says that before this ever happened, she had met a man on the street when she was roughly 15 years old, who warned her that she needed to be learning self-control for the plans she was to carry out later on in life. At that point in time, she had assumed this person to be Jesus, but later on in her life, after she had disavowed all ties with Christianity, she recognized his portrait in one of the Theosophical halls. He was one of the "Ascended Masters", Koot Hoomi. In her autobiography, she said:

> "He told me there was some work that it was planned that I could do in the world but that it would entail changing my disposition considerably; I would have to give up being such an unpleasant little girl and must try to get some measure of self-control. My future usefulness to Him and to the world was dependant on how I handled myself and the changes I could manage to make. He said that if I could achieve real self-control I could then be trusted and that I would travel all over the world and visit many countries, "doing your Master's work all the time..."

It is interesting to note, over and over, how many of these occult leaders had visits from unknown masters, whom they served devotedly. Blavatsky also had claimed to have been in contact with "Secret Chiefs" whom she described as inter-dimensional beings appealing to her directly through her intellect. Is it simply a fabrication, or something that truly happened to these, and other, disciples of the New Age movement? If they really were in contact with someone or something, was it truly a higher being that worked through them?

The story continues that Alice Bailey, in 1919, was contacted by another of these masters. She referred to him as "The Tibetan" and later, the name Djwhal Khul. This being communicated with her telepathically, urging her to record his teachings and spread them throughout the world. For 30 years, she maintained her connection with Djwhal Khul, which many speculate was nothing short of demonic possession. In all there were 24 books, most of which she claimed were written by Djwhal Khul and channeled through her. Alice Bailey felt that Madame Blavatsky had paved the way for her own work. One of her books was "dedicated with gratitude to Helena Patrona Blavatsky, that great disciple who lighted her in the east and brought the light to Europe and America in 1875."

At this same time, her eventual second husband, Foster Bailey, became the National Secretary of the Theosophical Society. Foster Bailey was a 32nd Degree Freemason, strengthening the argument that these two groups have common interests and goals. Alice Bailey continued her work with Djwhal Khul while delving deeper into Theosophy. Foster and Alice got married in 1921.

Foster Bailey stated in his own book, *Running God's Plan* that:

Modern esotericism is a new phenomenon in the western world pioneered by the Tibetan teacher, Djwhal Khul, working with H.P. Blavatsky. Again, this time working with Alice Ann Bailey, the same master teacher has provided the interim teaching needed for conscious entry into the new Aquarian Age. The study of this new teaching in the books published under that name of Alice Bailey is producing a revival of exotericism and a new technique for self-development, this time with the selfless goal of world service.

Notice the language running through that passage. It should sound familiar. The Age of Aquarius. Self-development. World service. Alice Bailey founded the

Lucifer Publishing Company in 1920, but the name was changed to Lucis Trust in 1922. The Lucis Trust of today claims that the choice of names was simply because Lucifer means "light-bearer" in Latin, but it is no coincidence, as the Trust to this day focuses on the illusion of Lucifer as an angel of light.

The goals of Lucis Trust, founded in 1922, were to set about the "Plan" that the hierarchy of these so-called Ascended Masters wanted to steer humanity towards. This plan included a "New World Religion" that focused on the evolution of man. There are rituals of magic meant to harness the energies of the universe to doing man's will – and ultimately the will of these masters.

Another of Alice Bailey's projects was her Arcane School. Here we have another revealing name choice! Through the Arcane School, students could enroll in correspondence courses in meditation. In the 30s, she set up World Goodwill as a benevolent (and highly influential!) society, that even to this day pushes for more power for the United Nations. She also set up an organization called Triangles which teaches a "Great Invocation" based on astrology and the cycles of the moon, to influence world events.

There are outlines on how to influence the world, through infiltrating and subverting education of the young, through popular media, through religion. Politics and economics have been enormously changed by the goals that this one woman and her organizations have set in motion. Even when the ultimate plan has failed, the efforts of the movement are still creeping forward, day by day, into our lives.

For example, one of the goals, as stated in *Running God's Plan,* by Foster, was a unified Europe. They tried using several river valleys as a unifying force, a binding factor in their attempts. During their time, a "sixth nation" was attempting to do it again, bring about a European common market and set about a New World Order. Again, we have the interests of Adolph Hitler lining right up with these guys. If we are to know them by their fruits, what does this say about the plans of this hierarchy of beings that were trying to, allegedly, liberate and uplift humanity?

Most of Alice Bailey's projects and societies were indeed successful. Both World Goodwill and Lucis Trust are recognized by the United Nations as international NGOs, or Non-Governmental Organizations. As we will see in later chapters, prominent members have changed the face of our lives today. People such as Henry Kissenger, John D. Rockefeller, Robert S. McNamara, and others have served on the international board of trustees of this society.

Alice Bailey's work has been largely influential in world politics and global economics. While most of us are not familiar with her name, or what she stood for, her work in the last century did much to further the goals of Luciferianism.

### Manly Palmer Hall – Grandmaster in the Illuminati?

On the other end of the spectrum of people influenced by the Luciferian concepts introduced, we have Manly P Hall. This man has been purported to be a grandmaster in the Illuminati, as well as a 33$^{rd}$ degree Freemason, by the end of his life time.

The word Illuminati means "enlightened" and it immediately calls to mind the way that Luciferians view the Lightbringer ideal of Satan. The Illuminati are directly connected with the Freemasons, being set up in the 1700s as an offshoot of that cult, folded into Jesuit dogma. The organization is very secretive, but there are traces that can be followed to show that it has survived to this very day. There are many groups that openly refer to themselves as the Illuminati, the Freemasons, or a few other groups, including the Ordo Templi Orientis.

All of these groups are working together, from different angles, for a common agenda. Manly Palmer Hall was a great student of the occult and familiarized himself with all aspects of the New Age movement, spiritualism, and these esoteric societies and mystery religions.

Manly P. Hall, born in 1901, grew up in Canada at the end of the Victorian Era. He was not traditionally schooled in a public classroom, but learned on his own at his grandmother's house. He showed a great interest and affinity from an early age for travel and the knowledge of other cultures. The beginnings of his writing career were largely travel based.

But then, in the midst of the roaring 20s, Manly P. Hall experienced a change of purpose. In his career on Wall Street, he experienced a life changing event: the shock of witnessing a suicide that was the result of stock market failures. Manly Hall began to devote his life to more spiritual pursuits and became enmeshed in the culture of the occult.

This brilliant man quickly grasped the power that was to be attained by following the paths of the Deceiver. The number of writings alone that Manly studied in his pursuit of enlightenment is astounding – more than 1000 works are cited in the bibliography section of *The Secret Teachings of All Ages* alone. This book was written and published by the time Manly P. Hall was 28 years old.

The aims and means of his secret knowledge are very clearly concurrent with Blavatsky's, and those of the Freemasons and Illuminati. It was that familiar Luciferian agenda —create divinity of mankind. His sources were as abundant as Satan's influence on the earth throughout history. A new world order needed to be cultivated and primed for taking over, subverting Christianity and keeping on track for the Great Plan of the ancients.

In fact, in 1934, he set up the Philosophical Research Society to further his goals and studies. That benign name does not readily bring to mind the actual purpose of this society, which is dedicated to the study of religion, mythology, metaphysics, and the occult. The pursuit that he began in the 1920s is still alive today in this society, the direct result of Manly P. Hall's beliefs.

Manly Hall dabbled in teachings from all ages and tried to find a common thread. He did not believe at all that there was one path, through Jesus. He toyed with everything from Tarot cards (he even designed a deck of his own) to astrology, to UFOs and extraterrestrial life forms, to ceremonial magic. He believed in the path of illumination, and helped set thousands of disciples on the same path he trod. He was truly knowledgeable and well versed in all aspects of the occult.

And Manly Hall did not just study it as a scholar inclined to dissect the truth from the false. He certainly practiced what he preached:

"The genuine Esoteric Associations always required that disciples prepare themselves for careers of practical service. The student was expected to attain to a state of unusual skill or proficiency in some branch of learning. He was then to practice this profession or craft as a means of ex-tending his sphere of constructive influence. He was to teach through example, enriching his chosen vocation with the overtones of enlightened religious philosophy. Thus, gradually creating a significant zone of influence, he was available for whatever task the Keepers of the Great Plan required. Practical ends can only be achieved by practical means, and the agents of the Universal Reformation must be sufficient for every emergency."

In this book, *The Secret Destiny of America*, Manly P. Hall outlines the Masonic aim in setting up the United States. These Illuminati, according to him, had goals in setting up our nation. He points to Masonic imagery on our currency and other images throughout the nation's history.

While one might be inclined to dismiss this all as wild speculation, the fact remains that, again, many prominent people have been incredibly influenced by Manly P. Hall's teachings. And further, the Freemasonry that he sought to bring to light, and reveal for all the world to see? Instead of disavowing the principles and beliefs that he taught that the United States was founded upon, they inducted him as a 33rd Degree Mason of the Scottish Rite, the highest honor and status you can attain as a Freemason. In fact, in his obituary by the Scottish right, he was called "Illustrious Manly Palmer Hall, often called the Mason's greatest philosopher."

This is a direct endorsement and praise of the same Manly Hall who wrote, in *The Lost Keys of Freemasonry*, that "...the seething energies of Lucifer are in his hands and before he may step onward and upward, he must prove his ability to properly apply his energy." We can understand then, that Manly Hall's words on Freemasonry are accurate, insofar as their beliefs and customs.

He tells us that they were to deny that Lucifer was their God whenever an outsider was smart enough to break through all of the secrets and figure it out. By the time you reach the 33$^{rd}$ Degree of Masonry, as Manly Hall had, you have to take at least 32 different oaths of secrecy. So, when the Freemasons tell you that you don't understand, or are jumping to conclusions about what they are really about, understand that they have sworn secrecy and to not reveal what they know. Why did Manly Hall get away with revealing his knowledge? Manly Hall hadn't taken any of these oaths when he wrote about Freemasonry. It was only after his work revealing them was done that he became a Grand Master.

### Continuing Legacy

> Why do the heathen rage, and the people imagine a vain thing? The kings of the earth set themselves, and the rulers take counsel together, against the LORD, and against his anointed, saying, Let us break their bands asunder, and cast away their cords from us.
> *Psalm 2:1-3*

These words of the Old Testament are still true today. The heathens are still raging, and the kings of earth and rulers are still counseling together against the Lord and his anointed. They are working towards a One World Government, trying to set up their own plan, and cast off the "shackles" of the rule of God.

There is a propaganda campaign to cover it up, of course. Their effort to discredit those who would shine the light on them is in vain. A little digging makes it plain that our values really are under attack. All you have to do is read where these New Age and Self-Help movements came from. Whether it's Helena Blatavsky, David Spangler, Benjamin Creme, Alice Bailey, or Manly Hall, they all tie together. There is evidence out there, if you look for it.

While there are many other disciples and adherents to this way of thinking we could outline in detail, there is only one more that we are going to focus on. That one was perhaps the most over the top, but still managed to be the most influential of all. That man is the self-proclaimed Anti-Christ, *Frater Perdurabo* ("I will endure"), the "Great Beast" Aleister Crowley.

## Chapter 6

# Aleister Crowley

To most of us, the name Aleister Crowley brings up very evocative images, usually brought about by popular culture's fascination with him. He is one of the most notorious villains of the last century. However, so often these images are romanticized and white-washed. Crowley's disciple Robert Anton Wilson, Ph.D. tells of a remark made to him by Caliph Hymeneus Alpha of the Ordo Templii Orientis, "There is no sense in trying to whitewash Crowley's reputation, Aleister spent most of his life systematically blackening it."

This was a man who was evil, who reveled in his own wickedness, and who defied God in every way possible during his time on earth. In truth, it is hard to discuss his acts and beliefs in polite society. The types of depravity that Aleister Crowley sunk into in his time on this earth are incredibly sensational to recount. It would be best to not speak of him at all, if it were not for his legacy.

### From Quaker Roots to the Beast of Revelation

Aleister Crowley was born Edward Alexander Crowley in 1875, to devout, pious Quaker parents. He claimed that his father, who read to him from the Bible daily, was the hero of his life. Unfortunately, that father died when Edward was only 11 years old, and Edward went to live with a brutally abusive uncle. Instead of leaning on the rock of God to get him through this time in his life, it appears that his mother's nickname of "The Beast" was what really took hold of his heart in his formative years. He embraced that identity gladly, as revealed in this account that Crowley wrote about himself in third person:

> The Bible was his only book at this period; but neither the narrative nor the poetry made any deep impression on him. He was fascinated by the mysteriously prophetic passages, especially those in Revelation. The Christianity in his home was entirely pleasant to him, and yet his sympathies were with the opponents of heaven. He suspects obscurely that this was partly an instinctive love of terrors. The Elders and the harps seemed tame. He preferred the Dragon, the False Prophet, the Beast and the Scarlet Woman, as being more exciting. He reveled in the descriptions of torment. One may suspect, moreover, a strain of congenital masochism. He liked to imagine himself in agony; in particular, he liked to identify himself with the Beast whose number is the number of a man, six hundred and three score six. One can only conjecture that it was the mystery of the number which determined this childish choice.
> *The Confessions of Aleister Crowley*

Being independently wealthy as the result of an inheritance, young Edward was free to set off to college at Trinity College, Cambridge. There, he changed his name, opting for "Aleister", playing off of his middle name, Alexander. He specifically chose an odd spelling of that name, that in English, Hebrew, and Greek Kabbalah numerology, the number of his name comes up to be 666.

The abused child had become a man and was finally living on his own. He showed a great intellect, and was actually enrolled as a student of Moral Sciences. He began to pursue his own interests, which ranged from the seemingly harmless, like chess and mountaineering, to the much more depraved. He began to experiment with sexual activities, having little regard for the rules of morality, but doing whatever pleased him. He began his writing at this period in life, and his first published poems were basically explorations of his sexual experimentation at the time.

As the result of one such encounter, Aleister's self-destruction became even more sinister as he began to devour almost anything dealing with the occult. He read books on alchemy and magic, and lost all interest in his studies, dropping out despite having a high grade and being on target to graduate soon. Worst of all, he began to develop his own moral philosophy, which he would actively spread to others:

> Before I touched my teens, I was already aware that I was THE BEAST whose number is 666. I did not understand in the least {XI} what that implied; it was a passionately ecstatic sense of identity.

> In my third year at Cambridge, I devoted myself consciously to the Great Work, understanding thereby the Work of becoming a Spiritual Being, free from the constraints, accidents, and deceptions of material existence.

I found myself at a loss for a name to designate my work, just as H. P. Blavatsky some years earlier. "Theosophy", "Spiritualism", "Occultism", "Mysticism", all involved undesirable connotations.

After leaving the university life to follow his own pursuits, he began to pursue his self-proclaimed path as the "Anti-Christ" in earnest. He was inducted into the Golden Dawn Society. The Golden Dawn Society, like the Theosophists and the Freemasons, is a group of occultists who were (and are, to this day) overtly practicing magic and have been a major influence on 20th Century (and beyond) fascination with the occult. As Crowley began to pursue his love affair with the occult, it only served to reinforce his desires to live a life of absolute moral abandon.

He began to practice not only "white magic" but also "black magic" with some of his associates of the Golden Dawn. He started experimenting with drugs, and began on a decade of traveling the world and learning more about the occult. This prepared him for contact with the ancient Egyptian "god" Horus, which he claimed spoke through him to deliver his most important contribution to the moral depravity that we see in the world today, *The Book of the Law*.

Like Blavatsky and Bailey before him, Aleister claimed that he was contacted and directed by third parties which spoke through him and served as his master. This was in 1904. Crowley had a communication with what he called an extraterrestrial being named Aiwass who brought him into contact with Horus, through his pregnant wife. He undertook a channeling operation, based on ritualistic contact with these and other entities via his wife. *The Book of the Law* declared that the slain and risen god (who else could that be but Jesus?) had stepped off the throne. He said that a new god, the crowned and conquering child was taking his place.

The rest of Aleister Crowley's life can be summed up as many years of depravity and outright service to demons, hedonism, and outright Satanism. Crowley's blatant disregard for morality is apparent, as is his love of Satan, through his prolific writing career. Everything he wrote was filthy, depraved, and delighting in wickedness. He was associated with many occult and magic practicing societies, such as the Ordo Templii Orientis, became a Freemason of great degree (or standing) in many of the different sects of that cult, and even established his own, new occult practices.

Aleister Crowley had no problems with the legacy he had created. He gladly vaunted himself as the wickedest man in the world. He claimed that Christianity was at an end, and that his own era, that of the Beast, was beginning. He advocated, amongst other things, a New World Order and establishment of a new morality and world religion and state of anarchy. His writing echoes so much of the Luciferian language we have read so far, another theme from the Bible. He says, "My eyes were opened and I had become as a god, knowing good and evil."

He set about trying to have a child that would fulfill his prophecies. He did many rituals to bring about an heir to the throne, to be the "crowned and conquering child." This failed miserably, despite Crowley's claims to godhood. Though he did have many children (many did not survive) through the multiple partners he had throughout life, all have tried to distance themselves from his legacy, and live life away from the shadow of this evil man. And who could blame them?

### *Influence on the World Today*

Aleister Crowley seems to be simply a deranged madman to many of us today. It would be so easy to dismiss him as such, too. He claimed to be the Beast and the Anti-Christ, and that seems to be grandiose megalomania, plain and simple. However, the main message of *The Book of the Law,* "Do what thou wilt shall be the whole of the law" has been adopted by so many today that we really cannot gloss over the man as simply a madman. Even if he was mad, he changed the face of the world, and we need to accept that this man's message needs to be understood and combated from every corner.

In 1931, *The Occult Digest* stated, "There is a great awakening sweeping over the world today. There are times when one fully believes that we are entering a new and more complete age ...? into the sunlight of 'Old knowledge made new'." Does this sound like something we should just dismiss and walk away from? Especially considering that Aleister Crowley's death did not diminish his influence on the world today.

If anyone influenced Nazism more than Blavatsky, it was Aleister Crowley's false morality. These people were clearly serving a power beyond their own ability to reign in. So many of them were simply mouthpieces for these demons and entities that are working to undermine God's work on earth, and subvert humanity into slavery, moving away from the love and freedom that we can find in Christianity.

Aleister Crowley is a favorite of popular culture. Artists like Led Zeppelin, Jim Morrison, David Bowie, Ozzy Osborne and Black Sabbath have been fascinated with him, writing odes to him and following in his footsteps. It is very important that we examine those who follow his teachings, even in a flippant or irreverent manner. This is nothing to play with.

In addition, through his various magical associations and organizations, which are still in existence, he lives on. Timothy Leary, who advocated hedonism and psyche-delic drug use to free the mind of slavery, was treated as a guru of the 60s. When you examine what Timothy Leary believed and taught, you can see how much he borrowed from Aleister Crowley.

Charles Manson also was a member of a group which was an offshoot of the Ordo Templii Orientis that Aleister Crowley was deeply involved in. Crowley introduced new magic into that group, based on homosexual depravity. He was the father of modern Satanism, and Charles Manson held to many of the same beliefs as Crowley. The Manson Family used drugs, believed in torture, and embraced racist ideals.

One of the greatest swindlers of all time, L. Ron Hubbard, founded his new age ideology Church of Scientology on the day that Crowley died in 1947. Anyone who takes a closer look at L. Ron Hubbard will learn what a dishonest charlatan he was, how he created Scientology specifically to make a mockery of organized religion. And he has. To this day, even though the evidence is out there, there are plenty of fabulously wealthy, elite, influential individuals who are members of his church and subscribe to the beliefs of Dianetics.

Some of these people come to the group knowing what they are getting into. But many others are indirectly persuaded to give Luciferian ideals a hearing, because the influence is so pervasive. Many of these people are deceived into believing Luciferianism, whether through his message, the message of New Age occultism, or some other means, is all about peace and love.

Crowley taught about finding yourself – how many young people go on journeys to find themselves? The whole of the law is "do what thou wilt" but then there is an emphasis on love – usually when you dig deeper this "love" is just sexual immorality, but it looks so appealing.

On the outside, a love based dogma, all about finding yourself and being true to your own divine spark seems so appealing and shameless. That's because Satan and his angels are masquerading as angels of light, of course. But what the true end of it all is the fact that there will be a brutal leader who will emerge to put an end to Christianity. Aleister Crowley is one of many, many disciples Satan has had actively working for his will in the world in the last century. What makes him especially unique is that he was open about this goal, and told everyone who would listen. We should not follow in his footsteps, but we should definitely take note of what he said.

## Chapter 7

# Charitable Organizations

We have touched upon some prominent names at the turn of the last century in advancing the cause of Luciferianism. There are many others that can be seen to play a major role in world politics and opinion. Often these groups are known as benevolent societies and operate under the auspices of charity work, seeking to unite the world and work towards peace.

We as Christians might be sympathetic to that goal, but we also understand that until God's kingdom has come, there will be no world peace. Those who achieve peace are those who walk in harmony with God, and as long as there are nations in rebellion to His will, there will be warfare. When all come to God, then it will be time to beat our swords into plowshares and see the lion lie down with the lamb, but not until then.

However, these peace seeking organizations, beginning with non-profit organizations that we will discuss here, and later on the overt political movements that have been made in the last century, are not in any way advancing the cause of Christianity. Far from it, they often do seek a One World Religion. This is a concept we keep repeating and is becoming very familiar by now. That religion is one that sets man up as a deity, worshiping of self instead of God.

We've seen that Alice Bailey's Lucis Trust and other types of nonprofits and allegedly benevolent organizations are often the backbone and front of choice for the Luciferian movement. When these organizations are clearly traced back to Theosophy, New Age movements, magic, or the like, they are easy to sidestep. However, there are many organizations that are operating under this guise of humanitarianism with a much more sinister purpose, that isn't readily apparent, as is the case with Lucis Trust.

These organizations are often ones we hear about on a daily basis. Do we need to check out every charity that professes to do good will? The answer is yes. We need to be ever vigilant, investigating and being aware of where our money goes, what we donate to, what causes are influencing the government, the airwaves, and public opinion.

> Dodd: ...But, they had to have something in the way of a rationalization of their decision to do everything they could to stop completion of this investigation, given the direction that it was moving. That direction would have been exposure of this Carnegie Endowment story, and the Ford Foundation, and the Guggenheim, and the Rockefeller Foundation — all working in harmony toward the control of education in the United States.

Of course, ignorance is no excuse. We do not want the Lord to say of us as he did to Hosea, "My people are destroyed from lack of knowledge." (Hosea 4:6) While this does have to do with knowledge of God's word, in God's word we have plenty of warning against the ever present war against heaven that is set on our earth, in the very hearts and souls of those inhabiting the earth.

### *Illuminati*

We have briefly discussed or alluded to the Illuminati throughout this book, and perhaps you are familiar with them already. However, it will help to remind ourselves of who they are and discuss them in greater detail. The Illuminati are one and the same as Luciferians. You can tell through the name Illuminati that they are working to "illuminate" the world. This goes along with Satan's light bringer aspect that he presents to the world, an angel of light. Officially on this earth, the Illuminati are represented in Freemasonry and other organizations like it, with the stated goal of bringing the light to the world.

The official group of self-proclaimed Illuminati as we know them today can be traced back to a group of "freethinkers" in Bavaria in 1776. However, they were clearly a branch of and inspired by the Freemasons, who are much older than that. The Freemasons claim to have their origins as far back as the original builders of Solomon's temple, while others say that this tale is simply allegorical. Either way, both groups are so shrouded in secrecy and occultism that uncovering the actual truth and separating those truths from myth is extremely difficult.

Have you ever met an atheist, or anyone, really, who insisted that they were a "free thinker"? It is common vernacular amongst the unbelieving, and if anyone who believes in God must be a slave and unable to think clearly. They hold that all thought should be based on science and logic, with no regard to traditions, authority, or dogma – which, of course, is what they reduce God's word to. This is easy to do if you do not believe in God in the first place, or are trying to set yourself up as your own God. That type of language has been passed down through the years, and no wonder. These are the same philosophies that form the Illuminati of history, and today.

Whether we are discussing the Freemasons, Illuminati, or Luciferians, do not be confused by the changing names. Do not be deceived into thinking these are completely separate entities. The record speaks plainly. These are all the same people. Their membership in one lodge often coincides with that of another society. Their histories are intermingled because they have the same aims, history, and goals.

The differences are often squabbles usually to do with organization or other political matters. Humans are prone to divisiveness, and even more so when everyone is out for themselves. The upper orders, those who have had to take oath after oath to protect the secret goals of the order, routinely lie to those below them, but these lies cannot always be hidden. This type of secrecy and deceit of the upper levels naturally led to unrest amongst the uninitiated lower orders, repeatedly leading to splinter groups and factions.

The Illuminati held enormous sway over European and American politics for the subsequent centuries. From the ruling classes and royalty in Europe, particularly Masonic lodges in Great Britain and Ireland, all the way to the town halls in the colonies and later United States, this influence can be seen.

Even our currency today has symbolism that has roots in Masonic tradition. Despite their secrecy in other things, the Freemasons readily admit that images such as pentagrams, the "All Seeing Eye" (which they say represents a deity, but cite Egyptian and Hebrew tradition alike when going into further detail) and pyramids are observable demonstrations of their reach. The pervasiveness of the Luciferians, specifically through the Illuminati and Freemasons, and their influence on the world is incredible, but it's there for us to see before our very eyes.

### The Rockefellers

Money is power, especially in today's world. And hardly anyone has more of it in the United States than the Rockefeller family. They truly rocketed to fortune during the Great Depression, when the rest of the United States was absolutely struggling to even eat. They used their money to take advantage of the stock market crash, and some posit that they even egged it on, profiting from other people's emotional overreactions and snapping up shares of stocks that were being sold in panic.

In truth, the bank balance only tells part of the story. There are many holdings that they control but are not actually the owners of. They are experts in power brokering. Some of the big companies they have held a controlling stake in over the years include Texas Instruments, Standard Oil, General Electric, Boeing, Delta, and numerous financial institutions. Their influence is truly too large to be recounted here, simply in the world of finance.

Despite this, the Rockefellers are not vilified as many rich are, but instead are known as great philanthropists. We hear of John D. Rockefeller as the man who made a fortune and gave half of it away. This family has worked hard for this image, contributing to such causes as the

Audubon Society and in land conservation in particular. This is, at times, caused by a simple sleight of hand – donations from one organization that they own or control, to another. In this fashion, they can completely control what is done with that money, and their power grows rather than diminishes. Their contributions are self-serving. They act as poignant PR for the family and foundations, even though they are really only donating money to themselves, to be spent how they want. There is no altruism involved.

The Rockefellers have founded many world changing institutions, or participated in them. These include (but are not limited to) the Council on Foreign Relations, the Trilateral Commission, the Bilderberg Group, the Asia Society, the Population Council, the Council of the Americas, the World Economic Forum, the Brookings Institution, the Peterson Institute, the International Executive Service Corps, the League of Nations and the United Nations. David Rockefeller is part of Lucis Trust's management.

Many of the actual political and financial organizations that they directly control will be discussed in the next chapter, so we will focus on the benevolent societies. The Rockefellers control an impressive group of non-profit or supposedly goodwill groups. Additionally, there are numerous colleges and universities that owe a great debt of gratitude for grants and funding from the Rockefellers. Education is a primary tool for molding the minds of not only the youth who pass through their halls, but by extension, anyone who comes in contact with those that have been indoctrinated in their ideas.

Through these means, this powerful family can control the media, control money, and control world politics. The family has been extremely friendly, to the point of outright sponsorship, of several anti-Christian groups. New Age religious figures like Reverend Moon and Maurice Strong are favorites of the Rockefellers. Some of the techniques employed by these New Age figures, like meditation, trance, and other mind bending activities, make the mind ripe for implanting suggestions and brainwashing.

If all of this is not enough to convince you of the danger of the Rockefellers and their influences, how about a quote from David Rockefeller, the current family patriarch himself, written in 2002?

> "Some even believe we are part of a secret cabal working against the best interests of the United States, characterizing my family and me as 'internationalists' and of conspiring with others around the world to build a more integrated global political and economic structure - one world, if you will. If that's the charge, I stand guilty and I am proud of it."
> *David Rockefeller, Memoirs*

### Carnegie Endowments

Andrew Carnegie has been called "the Father of American philanthropy." There are twelve Carnegie trusts and institutions. They deal with such broad scope as the arts, education, libraries, and social reform. These are all well-known and respected agencies, and have had tremendous influence on shaping the Western world. But what is really going on with the Carnegie fortune, and what are the goals and ends of all of this philanthropy? Many of us are reluctant to "look a gift horse in the mouth" - but we really need to get to the bottom of what is going on here.

In 1954, Norman Dodd was the staff director of the Congressional Special Committee to Investigate Tax-exempt Foundations. He had the unique opportunity to research exactly what many of these foundations and groups were up to. In an interview with G. Edward Griffin, he spoke out very strongly about various other groups that also are implicated in these nefarious agenda.

He tells the story of his investigations of the Carnegie Endowment for International Peace. Many of us know of Alger Hiss, who was President of this Endowment for many years, and the fact that he was tried as a Soviet spy, though never convicted, but later was convicted as a perjurer. While collusion with Soviets was a serious issue, there is plenty of evidence that the actual crimes against humanity and the American people that were sponsored by the Carnegie Endowment were far more insidious and goes back even further than even cold war espionage.

In order to study the Carnegie Endowment for International Peace, Norman Dodd selected an attorney on his staff, Katherine Casey, who was not sympathetic to the investigation. He chose her partly because, like so many people, she was a fan of endowments and non-profit organizations because of their public face, and the good they did. This was his effort to make sure that the investigation was not prejudiced against the Carnegie Endowment.

Dodd says that when Katherine Casey came back, she told such a shocking tale that eventually she lost her grip on reality, struggling to deal with the implications of what she discovered. She reviewed decades of minutes for the group, and uncovered some serious allegations.

The Carnegie Endowment **for International Peace** had from its inception in 1908, sought to alter the course of human history. They concluded there was no better way to do this but through war, specifically war that was global.

So, before World War I, the Endowment laid the groundwork to control the State Department of the United States. Once the United States was firmly entrenched in that war, they even sent President Wilson telegrams cautioning him not to end the war too soon.

There is also a clear cut history of the attempts (and successes) of the Carnegie groups to control education systems, and how subjects were taught throughout the United States and Europe. This indoctrination went on between the World Wars, and still goes on today.

### Other Groups

In the course of Mr. Dodd's investigations, he met opposition from almost every quarter. He says that they resorted to slander and lies,

> ...they had to have something in the way of a rationalization of their decision to do everything they could to stop the completion of this investigation in the directions that it was moving, which would have been an exposure of this Carnegie Endowment story and the Ford Foundation and the Guggenheim and the Rockefeller Foundation, all working in harmony toward the control of education in the United States.

Notice that other alleged humanitarian non-profits are also implicated here. For example, Norman Dodd claims that in a meeting with Rowan Gaither, then head of the Ford Foundation, he was told,

> "Mr. Dodd, we are here operate in response to similar directives, the substance of which is that we shall use our grant-

making power so to alter life in the United States that it can be comfortably merged with the Soviet Union."

All of this goes back to the agenda and conforms to the pattern already established. Alice Bailey addresses this in *The Externalisation of the Hierarchy:*

> "..educators and psychologists of vision in every country must be mobilized and the 'pattern of things to come' for the children must be intelligently determined. This will have to be done on an international scale and with the wisdom which comes from a grasp of immediate need and a far-sighted vision."

This power, coupled with the political and monetary organizations that they influence and control, serves to undermine national sovereignty, not only of the United States but of all nations. This sets the stage for one world religion as practiced and enforced by a New World Order under a global government. As we have already seen, this conspiracy is not only physical, but also spiritual in nature.

Alice Bailey's plan was laid out in plain view in *The Externalisation of the Hierarchy*. The setting up of a new world order will be one that will rise out of the ashes of the old world order. People as far back as Plato have discussed their desire to "recreate Atlantis." Whether this is literal or figurative, we are told by the demon speaking through Alice Bailey:

> "If this work is soundly done, then a world unity can be established which will produce right human relations, a sound world politic, a united spiritual effort and an eco-nomic 'sharing' which will bring to an end all competition and the present uneven distribution of the necessities of life."

If you ever listen to NPR, or watch public television, you are sure to hear the names of some of these charitable organizations. Though some of them may indeed be exactly what they claim, others are not. Consider that this is government sponsored news and information. We cannot simply take at face value the words that are being broadcast to us, especially if they are being influenced by the deep pocketbooks of the Illuminati, Freemasons, New Age movement, or other groups in direct opposition to Christianity.

# Chapter 8

# Government and Finance

"The world is governed by very different personages from what is imagined by those who are not behind the scenes."
*Benjamin Disraeli*

Through both monetary means and political action, the Luciferian conspiracy has made enormous strides toward their goals of a New World Order in the past century or so. The various groups and associations discussed so far had a cumulative effect on world opinion and in managing to worm their way into political systems and corrupt even the banking and finance industries to the point where we all, like it or not, are directly influenced by policy decisions that were colored by the Luciferians.

Many of the events preceding the United States' entry into World War I are at the center of this conspiracy. Some events in history are easily understood as Satan's work. For example, in Russia, the Bolshevik Revolution, originally seen to be the liberation of the Russian people, and then the subsequent coming of power of the Communists in Russia is easily seen to be a brutal, evil turn of the tide of history.

However, equally dangerous, and much more subtle machinations were being put into play elsewhere throughout the world. The United States government and people were manipulated by the Illuminati and became the source of great power throughout the world. The benevolent societies discussed earlier formed a perfect front to advance ideologies and concepts that otherwise would have been scoffed at by the average American. However, in a very short time, the United States became another tool for the Luciferian agenda.

### The Federal Reserve System and the 16th Amendment

"Whoever controls the money of a nation, controls that nation."

*President James A. Garfield*

When people discuss politics, they tend to gloss over the amount of power that money actually carries. Many of our world leaders were never elected to public office and do not serve in any government capacity, yet hold enormous influence over day to day life in a way that the government dares not dream. Baron M.A. Rothschild, the well-known Freemason, once wrote, "Give me control over a nation's currency and I care not who makes its laws." And this is exactly what they set about to achieve.

The establishment of the Federal Reserve has come under attack lately as being unconstitutional and contrary to the wishes of many of the Founding Fathers of this nation. Thomas Jefferson once said,

If the American people ever allow private banks to control the issuance of their currency, first by inflation, and then by deflation, the banks and the corporations that will grow up around them will deprive the people of all property until their children wake up homeless on the continent their father's conquered...I believe that banking institutions are more dangerous to our liberties than standing armies...The issuing power should be taken from the banks and restored to the Government, to whom it properly belongs.

Amongst even our founding fathers were Illuminati as well. Notable influences like Alexander Hamilton and the Federalists argued for a strong central government to the extreme that some criticized them as being royalists. One of their goals was put into action - the first Bank of the United States. It did not last for very long, because Jefferson felt it was unconstitutional and refused to renew its charter, the idea was worked steadily towards for over a century when it was finally reestablished.

Five years later, a Second Bank of the United States was chartered, in part to deal with the instability and inflation that the War of 1812 had wreaked on the United States economy. That charter was allowed to lapse when its twenty years were up, however, and it was not until during and after the Civil War that the Illuminati again found the economic and political climate ripe for con-tinuing their economic agenda. A federal income tax was enacted to help the Union finance the Civil War in 1861, and despite its repeal, a new, improved version was put in place in 1862. It was a temporary measure that would expire in 1866, however, and was not a long term tax.

The first peace time tax of the sort was established in 1895, however it was challenged in the courts and the logistics of handling and establishing how to deal with the tax made it impractical to act upon a national income tax at that point in time. However, these men are like their father the devil, and believe they are wiser than all around them, including God. Their lust for money and power is all consuming, and they were not to be put off very long in their pursuit.

This was a time of great fluctuation in American banking, and several small panics of various types plagued Wall Street. As a result, bankers were being persuaded gradually, by personalities such as Paul Warburg (whose company Kuhn, Loeb, and Co's Liberty Loans helped to finance the United States entry into World War I at the same time that his brother similarly helped finance Germany). Warburg wrote "A Plan for a Modified Central Bank", and Jacob Schiff, another partner in that group warned that "unless we have a central bank with adequate control of credit resources, this country is going to undergo the most severe and far reaching money panic in its history."

In 1907, this all culminated in a pivotal moment. The Illuminati acted upon it with an astonishing immediacy and efficacy that reflects the fact that this was all the result of their groundwork. There was a panic in the banking industry when the stock market fell almost 50% from the previous year, and many runs on banks and financial institutions were occurring. Whether the panic was engineered by the Illuminati, or immediately capitalized on, the result was the same – a strengthened stronghold on the American economy.

J.P. Morgan, financier, Illuminati, and businessman, held an enormous amount of financial power, buying out Carnegie's share in the US Steel Corporation, financing John Davison Rockefeller Senior's Standard Oil, and controlling the railways of the nation at a time when the railways were the lifeline of the economy. The fate of the nation's economy lay in the fate of a very few, but Morgan and Rockefeller, both prominent Illuminati, controlled more than any. Morgan later served as England's financial agent in the United States during the World Wars.

In response to the Banker's Panic of 1907, J.P. Morgan personally swept in and saved the day by backing the banking industry with his own personal fortune. He convinced several other prominent bankers to do the same and became the hero of Wall Street. While this averted the temporary crisis, it also gave the Illuminati an opening to secure their hold on American money and banking.

The Aldrich-Vreeland Act set up the National Monetary Commission in 1908. From this point onward, all banking issues would have to go through this Illuminati controlled body before making it to the greater floor for approval. As a result of this Act, Nelson Aldrich, Rhode Island Senator, and other members of the Commission went on a tour of Europe looking for answers to the banking crisis. Nelson Aldrich was later was to become father-in-law to John D. Rockefeller, Jr., and Nelson Rockefeller (Vice President under Gerald Ford) was named after him.

In addition to this trip, Aldrich held a secret meeting off the coast of Georgia on Jekyll Island. This was a very elite few of the most powerful bankers in the nation. In attendance were Aldrich, Jacob Schiff, J.P. Morgan, A. P. Andrew (Assistant Secretary of the Treasury Department), Paul Warburg, Frank A. Vanderlip (James Stillman's successor as president of the National City Bank of New York), Henry P. Davison (senior partner of J. P. Morgan Company), Charles D. Norton (president of the Morgan-dominated First National Bank of New York), and Benjamin Strong (also representing J. P. Morgan).

B.C. Forbes, of *Forbes Magazine*, wrote years later:

> Picture a party of the nation's greatest bankers stealing out of New York on a private railroad car under cover of darkness, stealthily riding hundreds of miles South, embarking on a mysterious launch, sneaking onto an island deserted by all but a few servants, living there a full week under such rigid secrecy that the names of not one of them was once mentioned, lest the servants learn the identity and disclose to the world this strangest, most secret expedition in the history of American finance. I am not romancing; I am giving to the world, for the first time, the real story of how the famous Aldrich currency report, the foundation of our new currency system, was written.

Out of this secret meeting would come the basis of what we know today as the Federal Reserve System. For two years the proposal was debated, in part because Congress knew that Taft would veto it immediately. On the other hand, Woodrow Wilson was an Illuminati approved and controlled candidate who had the ability to get this legislation passed into law, as well as the 16th Amendment.

In 1913, Woodrow Wilson proposed some revisions to the bills that would make the transition easier and more palatable to the public, like changing wording from "central banking" - which the public feared – to "Federal Reserve" which sounded as if this was to be a public bank. In reality, however, this was no governmental agency at all. Even today, many do not understand that the Federal Reserve Banks are privately owned, not a public institution. The nation's money system was now squarely in the hands of the Illuminati controlled banking interests.

At the same time the 16<sup>th</sup> Amendment was passed into law. If you are not familiar with Constitutional Law, this is the Amendment that allows for the collection of a national income tax. As mentioned earlier, there had been an income tax during the Civil War. In 1894, there had been an attempt at another income tax, but the courts found that income gained from property and some other taxes were unconstitutional because they were unapportioned direct taxes. The 16th Amendment removed that impediment and made collecting income taxes far more easy and practical.

The rich Illuminati were largely unaffected by the new taxes, cordoning off their earnings into tax-exempt non-profits such as the Carnegie Endowment, Rockefeller Foundation, W. K. Kellogg Foundation, and Pew Memorial Trust. Again, these names should sound very familiar to the readers, because they are still very much in operation, and their very existence is one of the loopholes that allowed the Illuminati to operate without paying excessive taxes, while the poor and middle class of America began to feel the true shackles of government on them.

Today the average middle class American gives more of their income to the government than a feudal peasant. While there are many different opinions and ways to approach tax reform, and that is not the purpose here, it still deserves mention. It is plainly evident by the way history has played out that in fact the very people who met together on that island in Georgia over a century ago knew what they were doing and how best to protect their own holdings even as they made moves to begin collecting the fruits of the labor of the rest of the United States.

### World War I

During the establishment of the Federal Reserve System and the passage of the 16th Amendment in the United States, there was unrest half a world away. World War I started in 1914, although it would be another three years until we entered the conflict. Many have suggested that the big moves in 1913, establishing the income tax and the Federal Reserve System, are indications that the United States was preparing for a war effort. It does tie in neatly with the Carnegie Endowment's efforts to push the United States into the war, and their communications with Wilson urging him not to win the war too quickly.

What the Luciferian agenda stood to gain from the United States getting involved in WWI – beyond the deaths of more innocents on both sides – becomes clear when we look at the aftermath of this war. For the first time, the United States, who had been staunchly neutral in any European conflicts up until that point, was drawn into world politics. The end of the war signaled the beginning of the prototype for a New World Order.

The League of Nations was Woodrow Wilson's brainchild, and he presented the idea of a peacekeeping body that would strive for world peace. It was formed seemingly with the noble goal of preventing another World War from ever occurring. This was laughable, since the terms of the Treaty of Versailles were widely criticized and known to be a setup for failure. The Treaty was denounced as unattainable for the Germans, who had been required to make restitution for their part in the war. It was understood that this was nothing more than a 20 year truce.

Furthermore, the people of the United States were not ready yet to get that involved in European conflicts.

Ironically, through the efforts of such people as Henry Cabot Lodge, the United States did not join the League of Nations, despite the idea being our own President's workings. Instead, the United States formed separate treaties with Germany and Austria. The League continued to exist until 1946 when the United Nations was established, but it was a failure on the part of the Illuminati towards their New World Order.

However, there were enormous gains made in the Luciferian agenda around this time period. When men are scared, it is a perfect time to start infringing on their liberties, little by little, so that they become slaves of the state. This is exactly what began happening in the United States in many ways. A nation that was established and for over a century had maintained a cool neutrality in world politics was now a major player. The sleeping giant had been awakened. The United States had great political power. To establish a New World Order uniting all nations under one government, one religion, and one monetary system, the United States was vital.

Towards the end of the War, the Bolshevik Revolution caused Russia to drop out of the war. The war had weakened the nation internally, and this provided a perfect opportunity for revolt. Karl Marx's views were the rallying point of the Bolsheviks. Under the guise of freeing the people, the Bolsheviks set about overthrowing the government of Russia and setting up their own brutal totalitarian regime.

Karl Marx's ideas were Luciferian poison. He is reported by history to be a brilliant but idealistic atheist, well-meaning but misguided. His own writings suggest otherwise. Consider, for example, statements such as these that Marx wrote in his poetry:

Then I will be able to walk triumphantly.
Like a god, through the ruins of their kingdom
Every word of mine is fire and action.
My breast is equal to that of the creator.

These are the words of someone who acknowledges that there was a creator, and considers himself a peer. In *The Player,* Marx writes:

The hellish vapors rise and fill the brain,
Till I go mad and my heart is utterly changed.
See this sword? The prince of darkness sold it to me.
For me beats the time and gives the signs.
Ever more boldly I play the dance of death.

And lastly, in his poem, *The Pale Maiden,* Marx writes:

Thus heaven I've forfeited, I know it full well.
My soul, once true to God, is chosen for hell.

If you want to see what it looks like when the Luciferians get their way, look no further than Soviet Russia. What began as a seemingly freedom-driven venture almost immediately turned absolutely brutal, particularly when it came to stamping out all vestiges of Christianity in the new nation. Lenin was adamant about that, and thousands of Russian Orthodox clergy and lay people were killed simply for the fact of their adherence to their religion. His successor, Stalin, made Lenin look kind and benign by comparison. Stalin was known for his pathological lack of concern for the people he ruled, treating them literally as cannon fodder in any conflict that arose.

The establishment of the USSR by 1922 was in direct accordance with Luciferian ideals, then. The existence of this nation would set the stage for the coming Cold War that followed directly after World War II.

### The Great Depression and the New Deal

Following World War I, the United States enjoyed a time of relative prosperity. The Roaring 20s were fueled by the Federal Reserve, which began expanding the money supply. The market seemed to be the place to put your money, as there were enormous profits to be made during this booming era. And then came Black Monday, when stock market prices fell by 90%.

Interestingly, most of the Illuminati were unharmed by the stock market crash, having invested in gold and silver in the year prior. Many, like the Rockefellers, were actually able to profit off of the tragedy, buying stocks at an all-time low.

Louis McFadden, Chairman of the House Banking and Currency Committee, was already under the belief that our own Federal Reserve had in part financed the Bolshevik Revolution. After the stock market crash, he repeatedly called for conspiracy charges to be brought against the Board of Governors of the Federal Reserve. He charged that the crash "was not accidental. It was a carefully contrived occurrence. ... The international bankers sought to bring about a condition of despair here so that they might emerge as rulers of us all."

While many did not listen to the wisdom of this Congressman (who died a mysterious death after a banquet in Washington shortly thereafter) one truth he told was undeniable. The Crash was devastating to the people of this country. Thousands of banks and individuals were bankrupt, and between 1929 and 1933 millionaires suddenly found themselves without food to eat. It was a desperate time for our nation. The result was a people who needed the government to save them.

Enter Franklin D. Roosevelt and the New Deal. This was the plan that would save our nation. The theme is repeated again —a plan that on the surface is for the good of mankind that eventually forces them to become slaves. In the New Deal, the seeds of today's welfare state were sown.

In 1933, by order of President Roosevelt, the design of the one dollar bill was changed. There are many symbols on this new currency, and they appear to be of Illuminati origin. While many disagree on the exact meaning of this symbolism, there is no doubt that it bears a lot in common with Freemason and Illuminati symbols that are commonly used.

To discuss one example, on the back, there is an unfinished pyramid with an eye at the top. At the base of a 13-story pyramid, the year 1776 is written in Roman Numerals. While it would seem logical that this is a reference to the signing of the Declaration of Independence, it is also an important date to the Illuminati. May 1, 1776 was the founding of the Order of Illuminati that began in Bavaria.

### World War II

"National Socialism will use its own revolution for establishing a new world order."
*Adolph Hitler*

Understanding that World War II was the work of Satan takes no persuasion. What occurred during World War II is now used as the illustration of the depths of depravity that humans will sink to with nothing but a little societal pressure. And we have already discussed how Hitler was in search of godhood for himself, believing he could tap into the dark powers and make himself into more than a mere mortal.

Adolf Hitler and Nazism were heavily influenced by the Theosophists and the concept of man as a god. This time, even more than in World War I, the world was truly turned upside down by the Great Beast. Since Blavatsky, the "Mother of the New Age" was such an influential person in Hitler's life, it follows that Nazism and the New Age movement should have a lot of similarities. Constance Cumbey, among others, has noted the parallels, including Aryanism, the master race, and a hatred of the Jews.

There are references in Alice Bailey's works, as well, that claim that the Jews had forfeited their rights and how the Messiah would not be Jewish. These writings insisted that the Jews had to go through "fires of purification", and that Zionist pushes to regain the Holy Land were to be fought at all costs. One of Hitler's goals, as well, was the quest for the Holy Grail. Many people would dismiss this as simple evidence of the man's insanity; however, he was, like the New Age movement, the Templars (the predecessors of the Freemasons), searching for transcendental awakening.

Drug use plays a big part in Hitler's history, as well as that of those seeking enlightenment and the expansion of the consciousness. In fact, Hitler used so many drugs (reportedly 70 or more at one point) to control his consciousness and health that it is actually entirely possible that he was simply led about by the Illuminati, rather than in full control of the agenda he was furthering. The use of drugs as a catalyst in consciousness expansion has long been a part of the new age movement. There was even an SS expedition to Tibet in 1938 and 1939, to study the culture of this land where so many of the New Age elite have claimed to find enlightenment.

As we've already seen, so called benevolent societies really pushed the conflict of World War I on the United States. WWII was no different. The Treaty of Versailles basically set the stage for World War II, and racial and nationalistic tensions were fanned as well. The rise of Nazi Germany was funded and pushed by those that definitely appear to be the Illuminati elite. One interesting development that happened after the United States entered the war was that the practice of withholding began, which made it much easier for the common man to not notice he was being taxed at all.

The Council on Foreign Relations (CFR) is an important mover in this point in world history. This (non-governmental) group was established as early as World War I, to advise Woodrow Wilson on how best to deal with post-war Germany and the peace treaties involved. It was headed by Woodrow Wilson's closest advisor and liaison to the Illuminati, Colonel Edward M. House. In 1939, the CFR published a secret document advising the US State Department how best to deal with the turbulence in Europe. This document, *War and Peace Studies*, was funded completely by the Rockefeller Foundation.

The CFR, along with its sister organization in Great Britain, the Royal Institute of International Affairs, has remained to this day a powerful influence on American foreign policy. So many important people in American life have been members of this Council that it would be impractical to name them all. Presidents and statesmen such as Dwight Eisenhower, Gerald Ford, Bill Clinton, and Henry Kissinger have all been part of this group. As well, celebrities who greatly influence public opinion, like Oprah Winfrey, Carl Sagan, and Tom Brokaw, are amongst their roster. And of course, the ever present Rockefellers and other prominent members of the Illuminati are always there, controlling the scenes with their influence and money.

Franklin D. Roosevelt, a 32$^{nd}$ Degree Mason and our President at the time of World War II, abided by the wishes of the CFR. It is now well known that this alleged protector of the people knew in advance about the attack on Pearl Harbor that galvanized public opinion and launched us into the war. What were a few lives when the whole world was at stake? There is also a paper trail leading back to American and British bankers that funded Hitler's movements in the war. Unbelievably, there may have been even further evil afoot than anyone realized in World War II.

The aftermath of World War II is when the biggest strides toward a New World Order were truly made. At this point in time, the unsuccessful League of Nations was disbanded, and the more powerful United Nations was set up. Suddenly, the United States, who had for years proclaimed their sovereignty and neutrality, was entering themselves into a governing body for the whole world.

The United Nations has a direct relationship with several of the aforementioned Luciferian institutions and groups. A few examples are the Lucis Trust, Rockefeller Foundation, and Carnegie Endowments. Many Luciferian and Illuminati groups enjoy special status on United

Nations Economic and Social Council, in particular, but other Councils within that governing body that seeks to control the entire world as well.

The beginnings of a One World Currency were set up at this time. The United Nations Financial and Monetary Conference, also known as the Bretton Woods conference after the New Hampshire town it was held in, was directly responsible for huge strides in this direction. As a result, The International Monetary Fund (IMF) was set up, wherein wealthy nations contributed to a pool and needy nations were able to borrow from it at need. Also, the World Bank was founded in response to the Bretton Woods system which tied the rest of the world's currency to the dollar and sought to use the IMF to bridge temporary imbalances in currency.

Doesn't that sound like the whole world would be united with one currency? And further, how much world indoctrination has taken place by the hands of the United Nations' allegedly peace keeping and humanitarian missions? It is hard to quantify something so far reaching. Third world nations are given aid, based largely from contributions from our nation's coffers. These people are taught to hate us. Just listen to any news item about the newest development from the United Nations. We are vilified at the same time as being the benevolent financiers of the world welfare state.

At the conclusion of World War II, many argued that the only clear winner was the USSR. They walked away with more territory and a strengthened empire. Worse, Stalin was arguably even more evil and more powerful than the Axis powers could even have dreamed of. While they had been temporary allies in the heat of WWII, it was now clear that the spread of Communism was a danger to life of freedom loving people everywhere. As a result, the United States became embroiled in the Cold War.

To fight against the Russian influence on the rest of the world, the United States adopted the Marshall Plan, which was basically an American backed reconstruction plan for Europe, hoping to keep Stalin's hands out of the political systems of these nations. Technically, the same aid was offered to the Soviet Union and its allies, though they declined. President Harry Truman also introduced the Truman Doctrine, which offered aid to Greece and Turkey to keep them from falling into Soviet hands. This ramping up of foreign policy was a major shift for American politics, and brought us ever closer to the New World Order.

The North Atlantic Treaty Organization (NATO) also was a result of World War II, as was the Warsaw Pact, led by the Soviet Union. The world was divided between ideologies of democracy and collectivism, communism and free enterprise. These two entities would be in opposition, gearing up an arms race that could have ended all humanity several times over.

During this time, a group of the elite of the world, named the Bilderberg Group, began meeting behind closed doors. This group, meeting for the first time in 1954, was comprised of many of the elite in government, banking, and industry. The meetings are always secret, never open to the public. All that is known is who attends, and the group of course has many of the names that we have established as probably Illuminati, Freemasons, or other Luciferian conspirators. A little later in 1968, the famous think-tank named the Club of Rome was founded.

### The Cold War

The Cold War lasted from the end of World War II until the Warsaw Pact dissolved with the fall of the Berlin Wall and the Soviet Union in the late 80s and early 90s. The state of fear that this set up throughout the world continued to make people the world over easily swayed, led by fear and willing to give up many things in hope of simply achieving peace and security.

Also, world politics were volatile and unpredictable. JFK was assassinated shortly after suggesting the United States government begin to print currency, instead of relying on the private banks of the Fed. The United States entered police actions in Korea and Vietnam. The nation who had never tasted defeat suddenly was unable to pull off a victory. This made fighting under the umbrella of the United Nations and NATO more palatable to the American public, and brought the world closer to a One World Army.

While the world was concerned with the mounting tensions of the Cold War, other abuses of power that happened over this period of time. In the 1970s, David Rockefeller founded the Trilateral Commission to bring North America, Europe, and the Far East together "to harmonize the political, economic, social, and cultural relations between the three major economic regions in the world (hence the name '*Trilateral*')." The logical result of it was to create three "super states" which makes joining the whole world together under one government that much easier.

In 1971, Richard Nixon made the announcement that the United States would terminate the convertibility of the US Dollar to gold, making the Bretton-Woods currency by fiat the currency of the world. This unilateral move was called the "Nixon Shock" and meant that no longer did the Federal Reserve have any constraints upon printing money. This move has been widely praised and derided, but essentially gave even more control and power to the monetary handlers, i.e., the private banks that are concentrated in the hands of a very powerful elite.

### 1990s

George H. Bush, former CFR Secretary, Trilateral Commission, Bohemian Club, and Skull and Bones member, became our 41st President. This move was much to the delight of the world's elite that had big plans for this presidency. It was truly time to make some big moves. In 1988, David Rockefeller gave the following endorsement for his candidate of choice:

Bush has the knowledge and has the background and has had the posts. If he were President, he would be in a better position than anyone else to pull together the people in the country who believe that we are in fact living in one world and have to act that way. . . .

From the fall of the Soviet Union until 9/11, the world was in great upheaval. The Gulf Wars and other conflicts led to the world over beginning to submit to the rule and authority of the United Nations in a way that never before had been acceptable. The term "New World Order" began to be used openly, especially by George H. Bush. In a famous speech made January 16, 1991, he stated, plainly for the world to hear, the plans that were ahead for the world:

We have before us the opportunity to forge for ourselves and for future generations a New World Order. A world where the rule of law, not the law of the jungle governs the conduct of nations. When we are successful, and we will be, we have a real chance at this New World Order. An order in which a credible United Nations can use its peacekeeping role to fulfill the promise and vision of the UN's Founders.

NATO, having no real reason for existence after the fall of the Soviet bloc, did not disappear as might have been expected. Instead NATO became even more strengthened and began to expand. Global cooperation became the buzzword of the day. The world was going to be a better place, and evil would be shut down as quickly as it rose up. Never mind that the very evil we were shutting down, often we had created in decades prior. Those types of questions were hushed almost as immediately as they were asked. No, the point was that the world was acting as one, for the betterment of humanity.

At the same time, the European Union was created, bringing Europe together as a super state with one currency, one governing body, and one voice. This was at first a doubtful prospect and a rocky road, but is reality today. And concurrently, in the Americas, NAFTA, despite heavy opposition, sought to unite the Americas as a single economic unit.

The Clinton administration was even more strident in their efforts to bring the American people under government control, and to surrender our powers and sovereignty over to the United Nations. People began to notice how we had to consult with the United Nations over issues that were clearly our own business, not to be argued in world courts. And as usual, the leading nation of the free world was held to unbelievable scrutiny and vilification while crimes against humanity went unchecked all over the world.

### September 11, 2001

Who does not remember the horror of 9/11? Everyone remembers exactly what they were doing and where they were when the famous Twin Towers of the World Trade Center was attacked. The horror of knowing that the Pentagon had been attacked, and then hearing another plane was grounded somewhere out there. Everyone's heart stopped, and the world was changed forever.

Many people have brought up some really challenging questions about the attacks on our nation, suggesting it might have been a conspiracy. The 9/11 Truth Movement has gained momentum enormously as the mounting evidence of the truth of that day comes to light. Whether it was truly an inside job or not, the answers we have received to date have largely only brought up more questions.

All of this brings us to the world we live in today. The past is easier to interpret, because time reveals many things that are hidden from us at the time. Political pundits are constantly arguing and trying to obfuscate the truth, or at the very least present their own ideas in the most favorable light.

We are hearing, daily, speeches such as this one by Gordon Brown MP, Prime Minister and Leader of the Labour Party at the Progressive Governance Conference, "I believe first of all that we now need nothing short of a world constitution for the global financial system."

What about this excerpt by Herman Rompuy, the first full-time president of the European Council?

We're living through exceptionally difficult times - the financial crisis and its dramatic impact on employment and budgets, the climate crisis which threatens our very survival, a period of anxiety, uncertainty and lack of confidence. Yet these problems can be overcome through a joint effort between our countries. Two-thousand and nine is also the first year of global governance with the establishment of the G20 in the middle of the financial crisis. The climate conference in Copenhagen is another step toward the global management of our planet.

These types of speeches are not simple rhetoric to be ignored. At the same time, shows such as the Alex Jones Show continue to gain in listenership. There are people that were previously from both extremes of the political spectrum that today have joined in asking questions that previously went unasked.

With the advent of the internet, the people that refuse to rely on the networks only for their news are fast becoming the new mainstream in America. Many believe that a mass awakening is on the horizon and the world as we know it is about to change dramatically. Where is it headed - in the direction of truth, or into the path of the adversary?

**Chapter 9**

# Pop Culture today

A t this point, you may have many questions. If the conspiracy is spiritual in nature as the Bible states, where is it leading? Are we truly as influenced by it on a daily basis as all that? Who is influencing the New Age movement of today? Is this trend dangerous? Why?

In Ephesians 6:12, we are warned,

> For we wrestle not against flesh and blood, but against prin-cipalities, against powers, against the rulers of the darkness of this world, against spiritual wickedness in high places.

The Bible foretells that as Christians, no matter when we live, we will be engaging in a spiritual battle, our whole lives. We need to be on guard for our souls, even more than our bodies. When we are in physical danger, it is much more easy to recognize and take action. The insidious nature of threats against our very government and the elite in high places can be tricky to recognize, let alone combat.

This is difficult, but not impossible. We must pay attention to how the occult is slipping into everyday life. Things that may seem harmless may be sowing the seeds of destruction in our churches, in our families, and in our own souls. Giving more attention to who we allow to influence us, and what their true motives might be, is at the heart of all of the message of this work.

### Abortion

One of the most heartbreaking of all battles that we as Christians are fighting today is over the death of the unborn who cannot even defend themselves. What was routinely looked upon as murder in times past is now a simple form of birth control. This is exactly as Satan would have it be. One of the first recorded commandments to man was to "be fruitful and multiply."

This commandment is seen in the very first chapter in the Bible, found in Genesis 1:28. While not arguing on whether having a large family is the best way to achieve God's work in each individual family today, Christians agree that the killing of innocent babes to further our own selfish wills is evil. Further, it can clearly be seen as worship of the self.

In the time of freedom from Egyptian bondage, God reinstituted the dedication of the first-born again with the Israelites. This powerful symbolism reminded the Israelites of the horror of turning their back on the lord. In Exodus 4:22-23, the Lord told Moses to tell Pharoah, "Then say to Pharoah, 'This is what the LORD says: Israel is my firstborn son, 23 and I told you, "Let my son go, so he may worship me." But you refused to let him go; so I will kill your firstborn son.' "

The death of the first-born was the final curse that God sent the Egyptians. The Angel of Destruction was sent to kill the first born of man and beast alike amongst the Egyptians, and any Israelites who did not paint the lintel of their doorpost with blood of sacrifice. The Egyptians figure strongly in Luciferian culture and beliefs. Even the Egyptians of the Bible were able to call upon their magicians to replicate some (but not all) of the Ten Plagues. Could this be because of demon worship? Perhaps these same entities that spoke to Aleister Crowley, Alice Bailey, and Madame Helena Blavatsky were involved in the times of Moses.

The dedication of the first-born is significant. The first-born is regarded as the Lord's property in the Old Testament. Today we are under a new covenant, but that should still strike us as worthy of our attention. Children are precious, our legacy to the Lord. Once upon a time the worst curse that could befall a nation was the death of their children, specifically the first-born. How many children today never even make it into the world before they are killed, surgically, coldly, and without thought beyond how inconvenient another person would be to care for?

### Rated R Lifestyle

Every day life has always been full of temptations of the flesh. However, even in the past century, our values have fallen so quickly that it's clear that something is undermining the very culture we live in. At the same time as these wars, governmental and economic upheavals have been changing the face of the world, the values of the western world have also been visibly crumbling. We have gone from a world where cursing and infidelity were shunned and even the appearance of such things was considered scandalous, to one wherein everyone does it.

And it's not just those who aren't religious. How many times have you seen someone on Facebook bragging about going out drinking with the buds, only to turn around and declare their devotion to Jesus? Obviously, we all have our temptations, and no book but the Bible can comprehensively cover how to live a life in harmony with God. But consider for a moment how the Rated R lifestyle of many Christians has even atheists calling us on our hypocrisy.

### Celebrities

One of the main tools of Satan is fame. Many people would do anything for fame, including selling their souls. Sometimes this is because they don't actually believe they have a soul, but other times it is an almost deliberate choice. As the Luciferians believe that they are gods, it makes sense that they would pay no heed to the warnings of the Bible, and that they must come to the Lord to receive forgiveness for their sins and sanctification. Instead, many celebrities either worship themselves, subscribe to various New Age or Post Modern ideals, or simply glorify pop culture that has already embraced these changes.

As we've discussed earlier, many very famous people were directly influenced after the time of Aleister Crowley. Led Zeppelin was obsessed with the man, to the point where Jimmy Page actually bought the Boleskine house he had lived in. Their songs are full of the arcane and obscure references to the worship of Pan (another guise of Satan).

Their fourth and arguably most successful album had four major arcane symbols as part of the album art. Each was a sigil that was to represent a member of the band. There was a fifth design, smaller, for a guest artist for one song. Each band member picked a sigil based on an ancient, powerful belief system that spoke to them. Of course not one of these sigils was Christian. They were based upon astrology, ancient magic, the legend of the lost city of Atlantis, or other mystical imagery associated with the Illuminati.

The Beatles also were captivated by the Luciferian agenda. Their trips to the East to study with mystics are well known. Their obsession with psychedelic drugs brought so much publicity and popularity to the movement that thousands of hippies and other practitioners of New Age religions and cults began following in their wake. As John Lennon said very openly and publicly,

> "Christianity will go. It will vanish and shrink. I needn't argue with that; I'm right and I will be proved right. We're more popular than Jesus now; I don't know which will go first - rock 'n' roll or Christianity. Jesus was all right but his disciples were thick and ordinary. It's them twisting it that ruins it for me."

Plenty of musicians, in particular, have especially espoused the Luciferian lifestyle. Though some will claim it is simply a "glam" stance, meant to boost sales, how can you really openly promote Satan, Satanism, and acts of evil while saying it's just a joke? Rock, especially the metal industry, is rampant with these groups. Some of them are very successful, too, such as Black Sabbath and KISS. Even their very names are Satanic, yet we convince ourselves it is just a farce, just a game, not harming anyone. Is that really the case?

Another, more insidious example is another glam rocker, Lady Gaga. If you have seen this woman sing, you know that she prefers outlandish costumes and attention seeking trappings. She came from a classical background in voice, but she rejected all of that in favor of singing on sex, immorality, and that Luciferian favorite, "human rights." While human rights are well and good, her songs take things a step further. In the bizarre and enormously popular video for "Born this Way" she depicts the birth of an "eternal" being that is at war with an eternal evil. The very words deny the ability of humans to be evil:

> I'm beautiful in my way, 'Cause God makes no mistakes
> I'm on the right track, baby I was born this way
> Don't hide yourself in regret, Just love yourself and you're
> set I'm on the right track, baby I was born this way...

Of course God makes no mistakes! However, there is so much more to following in the Lord's steps than "just loving yourself". The godhood of the self is very much alive and well in the rich and famous attention seekers of the entertainment industry!

The richest woman in America, Oprah Winfrey, is also one of the biggest influences on popular culture today. If you have any familiarity at all with her, she promotes all sorts of different New Age techniques, whatever fad happens to be interesting to her at the moment. She teaches that many paths lead to "the light" and that "the universe" does not care if you acknowledge God openly, as long as your acts are basically moral. She very consistently avoids any further open discussion that she considers "religious" despite her devout Christian upbringing and the fact that she says that her favorite hymn is "I Surrender All."

Most notably amongst Oprah's questionable moral leadership of middle class America is her endorsement of *The Secret.* Some have claimed that secret is actually the source of her wealth and prosperity. If you are not familiar with *The Secret*, it is a book and movie about the so-called Law of Attraction that basically means that if you wish for something hard enough, you can by force of will create the world you want.

This belief system has come under heavy criticism, because although there is a general, vague acknowledgment of a "source" it certainly does not refer to Jehovah. Often people who believe in these teachings will try and quote scripture, citing faith that can move mountains, or Jesus assuring us "Knock and it will be opened to you." But remember Satan also quoted scripture as he tempted Jesus in the wilderness. In fact, as Christians we are to take up our cross and follow the Lord.

Another source of celebrity influence that leads the world to Luciferianism is Scientology. L. Ron Hubbard, the creator of Scientology, set out specifically to openly mock religion, yet his is one of the most successful and influential religious organizations operating in the world today. Although the most notorious Scientologist, Charles Manson, would hardly win anyone over to believe in the good of the religion, others succeed in white washing this farce that openly ridicules the Holy Word. From Tom Cruise and Kirstie Alley to Greta von Susteren, these people broadcast their beliefs publicly and openly and many follow their advice blindly.

### Entertainment

Another way in which Luciferian ideas seep into our minds, indoctrinating and numbing us to their effects, is through entertainment. In addition to the earlier mentioned Satanistic and New Age musicians, there is a lot of music out there that does a lot to help brainwash us, whether by attacking values directly or obliquely. When you listen to the same thing day after day, it begins to creep into your way of thinking. Next time you're listening to something just because it has a "good beat" listen to the lyrics. Is this really the type of input you want your mind to be dwelling on, even at a subconscious level?

Many games that are on the market are clearly occult in origin. Dungeons and Dragons, that popular roleplaying game that once was accused of Satanic origins, did not die out in the early 80s. In fact, it has spawned many other similar games that pit the imagination of the player against fantastical creatures, and even gods. These characters are routinely magical in origin.

The game World of Warcraft, with 16 million subscribers, also plays off of these same concepts. While many would argue it's all in good fun, and you are actually fighting the bad guys, again, it might be wise to take a closer look at what it is that young minds are being exposed to on a daily basis. The simple fact that this many subscribers are regularly playing a game that features killing and magic testifies how widespread our infatuation with the occult and violence has become.

Other games, as well, fall under this type of genre. It isn't something that is done only by nerds in the back rooms anymore. These are just two of the most prevalent. There are other games that are far more serious, like Ouija boards and the like, where people try to communicate with spirits "from beyond" - which could in all actuality be demons! Even if the games themselves are completely make believe, they continually expose the players to the concept of magic and the occult and make these concepts familiar and comfortable.

Similar to that is the area of literature. Everyone has heard about Harry Potter and the popularity of those books. J.K. Rowling is one of the most successful writers of our time. Again, she argues that this is a book of pure fantasy, not based in reality at all. But we are at a younger and younger age, becoming used to the culture of the arcane, and familiar with magic being used as the means to overcome evil.

Another series of books that is targeted at young children is not even seemingly benign. That is the *Dark Materials* books. The first of these, *The Golden Compass*, was made into a movie, and there was a great outcry against the movie and the books. The reason so many objected to these books is that they specifically set out to indoctrinate children against religion from an early age. Parents who had children who were fans of Harry Potter, looking for a similar type of book, innocently bought these books for their children, not realizing that they were buying a book that intentionally promoted atheism.

And, of course, there is the ever present television and movie genre of entertainment. In addition to movie versions of the books mentioned, there are hundreds of movies out there that are all about glorifying the occult.

Popular television shows such as *Buffy the Vampire Slayer*, *Angel*, and *Charmed* don't just refer to these themes obliquely. They regularly show demons and other soulless creatures as beings that are active and approachable. The characters in some of these shows are witches, and portrayed to be heroes.

And it doesn't even have to be fantasy genres that familiarize us with the plans of the Luciferians. *Battlefield Earth* was a movie that thankfully tanked popularly. It was based on the writings of L. Ron Hubbard, and his fabrication of what the true purpose of man is, and his "prophecies" for the future. John Travolta, a Scientologist himself, unironically starred in that propaganda film sold as a simple Science Fiction movie.

*Star Wars*, that ever popular space opera, teaches us of an all-encompassing force that presides over everything and everyone. George Lucas explicitly has stated that he was intending to create a pretend religion. While we might laugh at those who write down "Jedi" as their religion, there are those people out there that have embraced this science fiction as reality. And further, George Lucas' disavowal of anything occult or based in truth has not stopped people from drawing parallels to the New Age movement and finding themselves more open and willing to embrace that type of belief system when it is presented to them in daily life.

Other forms of entertainment, rather than exposing us to the occult or other belief systems, promote lifestyles and political systems as being superior or equal to the Christian way of life. This is not surprising, but it is something that so often slips under the radar. How often have you watched a movie only to realize you are cheering for the philandering spouse, or the bad boy with a heart of gold?

On a daily basis, filth infiltrates the airwaves, in the form of morning Disc Jockeys on the radio, commercials, and internet conversations. Preserving the innocence of our children is all but impossible in today's day and age. What happened to good old fashioned wholesome entertainment? What sells is what is popular, which is more of the same. Our culture, in general, has been brainwashed into accepting the Luciferian agenda as not only normal, but preferable to the Christian lifestyle.

### Health and Wellness

Even our bodies have fallen under the influence of the New Age movement, Luciferianism, and other tools of the devil. When was the last time you practiced yoga? Have you ever taken part in group meditation? Did it even occur to you to consider the origins of the things that were being taught to you on a daily basis?

Chiropractic care has been understood to have many positive applications in daily life. The physical technique of the actual treatment that chiropractic has to offer has stood up to much criticism and scrutiny, on a scientific level. However, scientists do not generally delve into the spiritual training that often occurs in chiropractic schools under the guise of science. If they would stick simply to the mechanics of the body, it would be one thing, but there is a belief system that chiropractors hold in common, that is remarkably like Oprah's *Secret*, Aleister Crowley's search for deity, and Bailey's Ascended Masters.

Young chiropractors are often brainwashed into Post Modern thinking, believing that we all are conscious of innate intelligence which sounds fine until you start digging deeper. Each person is persuaded to listen to their own personal innate intelligence, as if they possessed deity themselves, and reach deeper to become all that they could be. The Law of Attraction is often taught to these doctors as part and parcel of their very profession! How disturbing is it that someone who you entrust the very health of your family might actually be trying to win you over through the manipulation of your body to dangerously evil ideas?

Another new branch of medicine, psychology is rampant with New Age techniques. Carl Jung and Sigmund Freud both had parallel beliefs in the origins of mental disorders. Freud, one of the fathers of modern psychology, sexualized all that went on in a human's mind. Jung, however, as a Freemason, believed in a spiritual nature that was at the heart of many maladies. He brought us the term "Collective unconscious" to describe a linked spirituality that underlies all of the world, human and nonhuman alike, and influencing all that we do.

There are self-help books of every type out there to teach yourself hypnosis and mental conditioning practices. The reason you have even been exposed to so many of these teachings at all is through the work of people such as Helena Blavatsky and Alice Bailey. Their work opened a path for the Western world to be influenced by the teachings of their masters, and prepare us to believe that all paths lead to the same end. That end is a Golden Age of Enlightenment for Humanity, a New World Order.

The aggrandizement of the individual is the religion of psychology as well as Lucifer. When a person embraces their own morality, and makes their own rules, they have set themselves up as a god. This is taught in therapy sessions across the world, an "I'm okay, you're okay" type of philosophy, masquerading as science. Do not be fooled! As Manly P. Hall stated:

". . . .there is abundant evidence that in many forms of modern thought — especially the so-called "prosperity" psychology, "will-power building" metaphysics and systems of "high-pressure" salesmanship — black magic has merely passed through a metamorphosis, and although its name may be changed, its nature remains the same."

While there is much to be learned from meditation, spending time in reverence and thought with God, the open-minded state that is achieved by techniques employed by chiropractors, psychologists, and transcendental masters are all similar. This is more than simple science. This is a religion masquerading as simple lifestyle changes for the better. The body might respond positively to calming the mind, hypnosis, and so on, but without the proper focus, this can leave us vulnerable to suggestion and belief systems that are not God's will.

Lately, even pediatricians have gotten into the act of indoctrinating people. They give child-rearing advice regularly, telling parents their opinions on such things as punishment, appropriate teaching materials, and feeding or nap time schedules. All too often, doctors are quick to medicate unruly children rather than let them learn discipline, arguing to parents that they will harm their children by teaching them self-restraint. Admittedly, there are cases that medication might be of benefit, and each of these bits of advice might be of value to a new parent, however, when a medical professional offers his or her advice under the pretense of being an expert, be forewarned. Doctors have degrees in medicine, not in child-rearing.

Look at the blossoming of behavioral diagnoses in the young today. Look how many children are numbed out rather than learning self-control. There is a growing inability in today's young to simply cope with daily life once they get into the real world. Is this really because they have some disease that needs medication? Or is a more nefarious situation happening, where our very children are being drugged out of their minds?

In general, when a medical professional abuses their station to promote their own agendas, it is time to shop around for another doctor. Take care that you do not fall into the trap of accepting spiritual and moral advice from your doctors when they disguise it as medical advice. This is one of the most dangerous ways that the agenda can seep into our lives, because we trust doctors to live true to their oath. However, no matter how safe it seems, remember, Satan's servants walk all paths in life, and hold great influence over many well-meaning people. Don't fall for it!

### Education

Being experts in mental conditioning and brainwashing techniques, the obvious path to indoctrinate a people is through the education system. Think back to your own childhood. Are there teachers that stand out as important to you, who made you want to emulate them, who made a big difference in your life? Odds are that you do have at least one or two of these people in your life. The young are so pliable and trusting, and the role of the educator plays a major part in a child's life.

Today's teachers have even more ability to shape the lives of children than ever before. Single parent households are more and more common, as are families with two working parents. Children of divorce also are in every single class. All of these work together to lessen the parental role and strengthen that of the classroom. A child spends hours a day under the care of these educators. Then many of them still are in school for a few hours more, in school provided after hours care.

The government and Illuminati recognize the power of this situation, and work day and night to capitalize upon it. The path of money is easy to trace. The Freemasons and other Luciferians contribute considerably towards our education and library system. Through charitable contributions, teachers unions, education of the teachers themselves, and other political systems, it is very easy to influence what is taught, and how it is taught.

And think - you will often hear those who are either directly serving Satan, or influenced by him heavily, cite the separation of church and state as a protection of our freedoms. If only freedom was truly their agenda! Hours of children being away from home, not even allowed to pray or hear the name of God spoken, unless it is used as a curse. This has to have a profound impact on the soil of the heart of our youth.

The separation of church and state is often only a way to leverage anything remotely Christian from being taught in the schools, or becoming a law. This, despite the fact that quite often, directly Christian laws are also promoting the common good. If there is anything remotely religious about it, it is evangelizing, unless of course, it is somehow covered under cultural or secular education.

It doesn't matter if your child has been taught at home to believe in certain values. If they are not socially acceptable according to the Luciferian agenda, you can expect to see them stamped out by the government schools' agenda. Christian teachers all over lament the requirement for Character Education – a thinly disguised way to teach children to be compliant, obedient, and subservient to the government first and foremost. And as more and more people expect the schools to not only educate, but also parent their children, the Luciferians get more and more disciples – stupid, naïve, uneducated, but easily led about by their government, upon which they are inextricably dependent.

### Politics and Money

We have already discussed at length how the Luciferian agenda has infiltrated both our monetary and governmental systems. There is not one aspect of daily life that has not in some way been influenced by their agenda. From the crops that feed us and the clothes on our back, to the money we use to buy those items, we have had countless encounters with evil, either directly or indirectly.

It is difficult to even discuss change or a return to past values without receiving great opposition. The political climate in the United States today is cultivated carefully by the Council on Foreign Relations, the United Nations, and other bodies that are clearly there to pull us away from God, towards a New World Order. Sometimes the political parties seem to only be slightly different, and that should not be surprising when we see how the Luciferians find ways to either infiltrate or corrupt people of all political persuasions. No matter how well-meaning a public official might be, the time when compromise with these people seems inevitable will come.

### Decline of the Family

All of this together adds up to a world where Christian families find it hard to find their way in the world. Financial issues are the number one cause of divorce in America, and we are in a financial crisis today. More and more are relying on unemployment benefits, welfare, and charity just to get through another day. Foreclosures and bankruptcies are at record levels. This is more than just a symptom – it is a method of destroying our faith.

It is so easy to be led astray by persuasive doctrines when you are desperate and everyone else is doing it. Depressed people seek comfort in inappropriate places. Even Christians find themselves turning to drink, drugs, and sex to numb the desperation they find. This is dissolving the family unit.

At the same time, one income families find it nearly impossible to make ends meet. The child spends more and more time away from home, under the care of government schools that have strong union and other agendas. The parents find themselves struggling to make ends meet, or bailing out other family members, or simply caught up in their own selfish needs.

"Fathers, do not exasperate your children; instead, bring them up in the training and instruction of the Lord." Ephesians 6:4 tells us. So often, fathers don't even have time to exasperate their children, because they are absent or so busy with their own careers. Mothers are in the same situation, thanks to social and economic pressures.

The state of the family is directly related to the state of the government. In today's world, where teen pregnancies, single parent families, broken homes, and other tragedies are commonplace, is it any wonder that Satan has found a fruitful ground for his army?

# Chapter 10

# The Bible, Prophecy, and the New World Order

The picture of the world today isn't pretty, is it? The Bible predicted that in the End Times before Jesus returns, the Word of God would not be taken seriously. People who have never read the Bible are taken as experts, and believed by the general public and given real attention. Scoffers and critics are seen as educated and wise, while those who have read the Bible, and are intimately acquainted with all that is in it, are dismissed as backwards and ignorant. What could be further from the truth?

John R. Rice, Baptist preacher and founder of the newspaper, *The Sword of the Lord*, summed it up very well: "I am convinced that the only people who do not believe the Bible are those who have not studied it devoutly and tried it thoroughly, and do not know the evidence in its favor, or who have a deliberate and wicked bias against God and the truth."

All of this criticism and wicked bias against God might be discouraging to those who are in Christ's army, but we should take heart. This is exactly what we should expect. Many Christians believe in the absolute truth of the Bible, to be taken literally whenever possible, while obviously the prophetic language is also understandable with a little work. We need now to discuss what the Bible says on the issue of the New World Order. If the Bible is what it claims to be, the absolute truth, it must be what is our standard for measuring all other information.

### The Truth

Why trust the Bible? What makes it so special, or different from any other book on earth? How do we prove that it is the word of God, exactly the life and soul saving document that we cannot live without? A short lesson on apologetics, which is another term for the study of the proofs of the veracity and authenticity of Bible, is in order. With a simple look at evidence, we can learn what sets the Bible apart from any other religious texts, like the Koran, Baghavad Gita, or others?

First of all, no book on earth has the kind of documented support the Bible has. Many of these New Age doctrines that we have discussed so far, and others like them, fall under the umbrella of what is being sold to the public as "the truth movement". Following in the oldest pattern of them all, these doctrines claim to supplant God's word in order to reveal some so-called *real* truth, as if that was in opposition to the words of the Bible.

It is interesting to read how in the Bible, this very turn of events was even predicted. Thousands of years ago, in various places throughout the Bible, God predicted a time when people would go after doctrines of demons and seducing spirits. In 1 Timothy 4:1, it states the following: "The Spirit clearly says that in later times some will abandon the faith and follow deceiving spirits and things taught by demons."

In 2 Peter 2 :1-3, there is an extensive discussion of these false teachers, how they have always been with us and always will, but especially in the end times.

> "But there were also false prophets among the people, just as there will be false teachers among you. They will secretly introduce destructive heresies, even denying the sovereign Lord who bought them— bringing swift destruction on themselves. Many will follow their shameful ways and will bring the way of truth into disrepute. In their greed these teachers will exploit you with stories they have made up. Their condemnation has long been hanging over them, and their destruction has not been sleeping.

And again, in 2 Peter 3:3-7,

> First of all, you must understand that in the last days scoffers will come, scoffing and following their own evil desires. They will say, "Where is this 'coming' he promised? Ever since our fathers died, everything goes on as it has since the beginning of creation." But they deliberately forget that long ago by God's word the heavens existed and the earth was formed out of water and by water. By these waters also the world of that time was deluged and destroyed. By the same word the present heavens and earth are reserved for fire, being kept for the day of judgment and destruction of ungodly men.

This is a powerful reminder that it isn't up to us to defend this book, God's word. Many people call the study of apologetics "the defense of the Bible." While that is a very descriptive term, the truth of the matter is that you and I don't have to defend this book any more than we have to defend a lion. If you open the cage, the lion will defend itself.

Understanding that the Bible is its own defense, we still need to study apologetics. This is not about the inadequacy of the Bible, however. It is for the purpose of strengthening our own belief and faith in the words of God. If we understand deeply how true the Bible is, we will know that our faith is built on facts, and nothing will be able to shake us. Knowing how to refute the lies of Satan is our duty as Christians.

We know, when we hold the Bible in our hands, that it is the word of God, preserved with amazing accuracy through the years. There are Biblical scholars who can attest to the purity of the translation and the devotion of the scribes who were charged with writing down the Old Testament so that it survived intact in such accuracy that is unparalleled in any other secular or religious text in history.

One of the most surprising things about the Bible is the sheer number of early texts, from a time when Christians were severely persecuted, and many were trying fervently to stamp out all traces of the religion. Usually, if a group of people were being wiped out, the best you could hope for is some obscure archaeological evidence, and some translations of rumored tales by interested scholars, watered down and changed by the filters of culture. None of this is true of the Bible. Despite all of the persecution and attempts to subvert it, the sacred word has been kept whole and unchanged throughout time just as the author, the Lord God and the Holy Spirit, have not been changed.

The historical record holds this up. When manuscripts are found, the translations have kept pure from the corruption of repeated translation. The early Christians kept records that tell us exactly what was going on in the climate at the time, which works were the works of the apostles and were understood to be divinely inspired. Even those rejected works of the Gnostics, so much like today's Illuminati and Luciferians, subverting and corrupting the word of God, did not pervert the purity of the message. Truly, some sort of divine, supernatural power was protecting these words, making sure that the message remained intact throughout the years, so that God's people would have the words within them.

Many people point to the different authors of the Bible, but we understand that fundamental fact. There were at least 40 different human authors of the Bible. It is plain that God used His followers as his instrument in communicating His Will to us all, but the pen that set it down, be it John on the Isle of Patmos, Isaiah, Peter, or any other author of the various books of Bible, was working the Lord's work. The Holy mind that spoke though different voices was the same, and even though the sentence structure might vary, the consistency of the message is clear. The human authors of the Bible were divinely inspired.

One thing that sets the Bible, the word of God, apart from the Koran, ancient Hindu or Buddhist texts, James Joyce's *Ulysses,* or any other book out there, is prophecy. Roughly a third or more of Biblical passages are prophetic. Not only that, but many of these prophecies have already had the opportunity to be proven. Even more are coming to pass day to day as we progress through time. This definitely sets it apart. The fulfillment of these prophetic scriptures does so much to prove the veracity of the words of the Bible, and establishes them as God's written Word.

God says in Isaiah that the prophecies are the proof of his word. We can know that our God is the true God, unlike the demons or false gods of idolatry that worshiped demons or Satan in another guise in Bible times, and today are following New Age, Post Modern, or Luciferian doctrines today.

> Remember the former things, those of long ago;
> > I am God, and there is no other;
> > I am God, and there is none like me.
> I make known the end from the beginning,
> > from ancient times, what is still to come.
> I say: My purpose will stand,
> > and I will do all that I please.
> From the east I summon a bird of prey;
> > from a far-off land, a man to fulfill my purpose.
> What I have said, that will I bring about;
> > what I have planned, that will I do.
> > > *Isaiah 46:9-11*

## The Book of Daniel

A perfect example of how the Lord's words have come to be is the book of Daniel. It was written roughly in 537 BC, and many of the words in it did not come to pass for centuries to come. The prophecy here is an excellent point of study for those who would discover if the Lord truly is speaking in the Bible.

Throughout the book of Daniel, there are many prophecies that have come to pass and that we are still waiting on. In chapter 2 of Daniel, he tells how that in the second year of King Nebuchadnezzar's reign, that king had a dream that troubled his spirit greatly, and he was unable to sleep. The next day King Nebuchadnezzar called his entourage of magicians, sorcerers, and astrologers to interpret the dream, and they were all too ready to give him an explanation, if he would just supply the details of the dream.

Nebuchadnezzar was no fool, though, and skeptic that he was, he only would hear the interpretation of the dream from the one who could tell him what the dream was that had troubled him so. Of course, the group of false prophets that Nebuchadnezzar employed was unable to do that, because they were not true prophets. Nebuchadnezzar became furious and had all of his "wise men" executed.

Daniel and his friends were next on the chopping block, literally. He asked for time, and went to his friends and asked them to pray with him for the dream and its interpretation. Divinely inspired, he was able to fulfill Nebuchadnezzar's demands. Instead of taking the glory, he told the king that the Lord was responsible for the not only the dream, but its interpretation.

> Daniel replied, "No wise man, enchanter, magician or diviner can explain to the king the mystery he has asked about, but there is a God in heaven who reveals mysteries. He has shown King Nebuchadnezzar what will happen in days to come. Your dream and the visions that passed through your mind as you lay on your bed are these:
>
> "As you were lying there, O king, your mind turned to things to come, and the revealer of mysteries showed you what is going to happen. As for me, this mystery has been revealed to me, not because I have greater wisdom than other living

men, but so that you, O king, may know the interpretation and that you may understand what went through your mind. "You looked, O king, and there before you stood a large statue—an enormous, dazzling statue, awesome in appearance. The head of the statue was made of pure gold, its chest and arms of silver, its belly and thighs of bronze, its legs of iron, its feet partly of iron and partly of baked clay. While you were watching, a rock was cut out, but not by human hands. It struck the statue on its feet of iron and clay and smashed them. Then the iron, the clay, the bronze, the silver and the gold were broken to pieces at the same time and became like chaff on a threshing floor in the summer. The wind swept them away without leaving a trace. But the rock that struck the statue became a huge mountain and filled the whole earth.

*Daniel 2: 27-35*

Daniel goes further with the interpretation of this dream. He foretells the four major world empires through the figure of the statue. The Babylonian Empire was the head of gold. The arms of silver represented the Medo-Persians. The belly and thighs of brass we can now recognize as the Greek Empire, and the legs of iron, Rome.

There is some disagreement amongst scholars about the iron and clay at the foot of the image, whether it was the reemerging Roman Empire, or a world empire of ten regions. The Bible clearly predicts a world government to emerge, filling the whole earth. The New World Order was prophecied as far back as Daniel's day, and further in the Book of Revelation. This new world order is destruction, but it would come with the promises of peace.

We should pay attention to these prophecies, because other passages in Daniel have also been shown to be truth. Daniel tells of the rise and fall of the Greek and Roman empires. From the time of Daniel to Christ's second coming, Daniel shows the rise and fall of the world powers. In chapter 8, the discussion and interpretation of Daniel's dream in the third year of Belshazzar's reign is significant.

> As I was thinking about this, suddenly a goat with a prominent horn between his eyes came from the west, crossing the whole earth without touching the ground. He came toward the two-horned ram I had seen standing beside the canal and charged at him in great rage. I saw him attack the ram furiously, striking the ram and shattering his two horns. The ram was powerless to stand against him; the goat knocked him to the ground and trampled on him, and none could rescue the ram from his power. The goat became very great, but at the height of his power his large horn was broken off, and in its place four prominent horns grew up toward the four winds of heaven.
>
> *Daniel 8:5-8*

This chapter is a detailed foretelling of the Persians and the Greeks. The ram of the Persians is defeated by the goat of the west. This is a vivid description of Alexander the Great's conquest of the Medo-Persian Empire. Alexander the Great is represented by the prominent horn on the goat of the west. You can see his reign suddenly cut off in the prime of his youth, when he was only in his 20s. Four generals, represented by the four horns were Lysimachus, Cassander, Seleucus, and Ptolemy. They came into power and divided up the empire. Lysimachus inherited Asia Minor and Thrace, while Cassander received Macedonia and Greece. Ptolemy's share was Egypt through Cyprus, and Seleucus cleaned up with the remainder of Asia.

While the language of prophecy is symbolic, after the events have occurred it is much easier to work out what has happened and the truth of God's word. This was written two centuries before Alexander's rise and fall. There was no way that Daniel knew what was coming to pass of his own accord. The Lord was speaking through Daniel, and his words are those of the Lord's.

### The Return of Israel to the Holy Land

One of the most powerful evidences of the Bible's truth and application to today's world is the return of Israel to their land in 1948. Throughout the Old Testament, the fact that the children of Israel will be scattered throughout the world, persecuted and despised and hated among all nations. The strange thing is that right before 1948, the very concept of the Jews returning to the homeland was almost unthinkable. After 2000 years, God's people that were scattered all over the earth, just like was prophecy predicted, come together. The British pulled out of Israel and all of a sudden, Israel is reestablished as the nation of the Holy Land. This happened all at once.

Compare the facts of the political situation in 1948 that resulted in the reestablishment of Israel's nationhood, with this scripture from Isaiah:

> Before she goes into labor,
> she gives birth;
> before the pains come upon her,
> she delivers a son.
> Who has ever heard of such a thing?
> Who has ever seen such things?
> Can a country be born in a day
> or a nation be brought forth in a moment?
> Yet no sooner is Zion in labor
> than she gives birth to her children.
> *Isaiah 66:7-8*

Even this is foretold in scriptures! This bizarre and unsettling, otherwise unforeseeable event, is told to us. Even in the New Testament, Israel is pivotal and important, even to the end times. You have probably heard many comments about the following passage:

> I am going to make Jerusalem a cup that sends all the surrounding peoples reeling. Judah will be besieged as well as Jerusalem. On that day, when all the nations of the earth are gathered against her, I will make Jerusalem an immovable rock for all the nations. All who try to move it will injure themselves.
> *Zechariah 12: 2-3*

Many scoff at the idea that Israel is of any importance, pushing for taking away parts of the nation for Palestinian national movement. A nation that was almost wiped out, is now 6.5 million strong, and world peace depends on that tiny region in the world. Everyone wants that land. Prophecy is coming true before our very eyes, in our lifetime.

The word of the Lord is eternal. Therefore, we should listen carefully to these words:

'This is what the Sovereign LORD says: When I gather the people of Israel from the nations where they have been scattered, I will be proved holy through them in the sight of the nations. Then they will live in their own land, which I gave to my servant Jacob. They will live there in safety and will build houses and plant vineyards; they will live in safety when I inflict punishment on all their neighbors who maligned them. Then they will know that I am the LORD their God.'

*Ezekiel 28:25-26*

The United Nations repeatedly condemns Israel, even to this day. They have never come out against attacking nations, but the Jews who are defending the lands that they came into in 1948 and subsequently successfully defended and won in treaties, have been condemned. More than any other topic that comes before the United Nations, Israel is truly sending the surrounding peoples – throughout the world – reeling. Through the actions of the United Nations, the entire world stands against Israel, but they stand firm against Satan's attacks, via the United Nations, the Muslim nations surrounding them, or anyone else.

When people argue against the condemnation of Israel, it is for very good reason. God has gathered Israel at last from the nations where they were scattered. No one should be content to receive the same punishment as the neighbors who malign them. The United Nations, the head of the New World Order, should not be permitted to speak for all the people of the earth. If we follow blindly by the lead of this supposedly goodwill organization, what will be our end?

### Hope for the Believers

But faced with all this, what should we do? If the battle is spiritual, then we must have victory spiritually. The only way we can have victory is the Good News. In Revelation 19:10, we learn that "the testimony of Jesus is the spirit of prophecy." So much of the Bible, roughly one third, is prophetic, and those prophecies time and again have been shown to be the truth. So we know that the end times that have been prophesied in the book of Revelation and in other parts of the Bible are truly coming to pass.

This New World Order is disturbing, and it does fall to us to guard ourselves against listening to these false teachers. At the same time, however, there is plenty of promise for their punishment and our own protection. We may live in troubling times, but the victory will be ours.

Remember that passage in 2 Peter 2? It continues with a strong warning, but also hope for us all:

> For if God did not spare angels when they sinned, but sent them to hell, putting them into gloomy dungeons to be held for judgment; if he did not spare the ancient world when he brought the flood on its ungodly people, but protected Noah, a preacher of righteousness, and seven others; if he condemned the cities of Sodom and Gomorrah by burning them to ashes, and made them an example of what is going to happen to the ungodly; and if he rescued Lot, a righteous man, who was distressed by the filthy lives of lawless men (for that righteous man, living among them day after day, was tormented in his righteous soul by the lawless deeds he saw and heard)— if this is so, then the Lord knows how to rescue godly men from trials and to hold the unrighteous for the day of judgment, while continuing their punishment.

This is especially true of those who follow the corrupt desire of the sinful nature and despise authority.

*2 Peter 2:4-10*

Noah and Lot lived through some of the most trying situations that the world has ever seen. The punishment God brought the world, as well as Sodom and Gomorrah, was not without warning, though. Neither is the time we are living in, and the end result of these times will be as indelible and final.

"Now is the time for judgment on this world; now the prince of this world will be driven out. And I, when I am lifted up from the earth, I will draw all people to myself." (John 12:31,32) Jesus spoke these words while he was still on the earth, but now He is drawing all people to himself. We should take heart, because God will rescue those of us who are faithful.

We have been told time and again, that God will reserve his punishment for those responsible, and those who do not stand up for what is right. It is up to us to hold true to His word, and not fall for those who would lead us into error, no matter how convincing they might be. The Lord even punished those angels who sinned. This is how Lucifer appears to so many. Neither he, nor his disciples, will escape God's judgment.

God "has rescued us from the dominion of darkness and brought us into the kingdom of the Son he loves, in whom we have redemption, the forgiveness of sins." (Colossians 1:13,14). The same joy that we have in our redemption and the forgiveness of our sins, can bear us through the troubling times ahead. Grace is ours, as long as we claim it.

Even if we once bought into the lies, or served the very purposes and agenda which are now revealed to us, we are told, "As for you, you were dead in your transgressions and sins, in which you used to live when you followed the ways of this world and of the ruler of the kingdom of the air, the spirit who is now at work in those who are disobedient." (Ephesians 2:1,2) We are no longer dead! We are no longer in bondage to those influences that once ruled over us!

This does not mean that we can never make the mistake of falling back into believing the deceptions of Satan, however. We must always remember to "Be alert and of sober mind. Your enemy the devil prowls around like a roaring lion looking for someone to devour. " (1 Peter 5:8)

Being alert and of sober mind is no guarantee that the world itself will not fall into Satan's hands, and that we will escape the End Times where so much grief will strike the world. But we have countless examples of faithful lives to emulate. God's perfectly preserved words are there for us to study and learn from, to grow in our faith and wisdom.

The book of Job tells us of a man who suffered more than many of us can even imagine. Everything he owned was taken from him, his children were killed, his friends asked what he had done to deserve such bad things in his life. His wife urged him to curse God and die. He refused to curse God, or turn his back on his belief, but he did cry out to the Lord. Just like us, Job was human, and could not fathom God's divine plan. He clamored for God to explain and to show why he, who had been so faithful, should be punished when he had lived his life right.

The Book of Job is a great comfort in times when we feel alone, when understanding of God's ways fails us. God allowed Satan to attack Job, and even points Job out as one of his faithful. God was using Satan's ways, and turning them to his greater glory. How could Job understand, thousands of years ago, how many millions of people that his faithfulness and questions would serve as a testimony to? God does work in mysterious ways, but remember, we, like Job, will be rewarded in the end if we stand strong.

When you are feeling weak in and of yourself to withstand the constant onslaught of Satan, which starts in small everyday temptations in your own life but works its way all the way up to a plan to truly subvert the world, creating Satan's New World Order, remember these words:

> Finally, be strong in the Lord and in his mighty power. Put on the full armor of God, so that you can take your stand against the devil's schemes. For our struggle is not against flesh and blood, but against the rulers, against the authorities, against the powers of this dark world and against the spiritual forces of evil in the heavenly realms. Therefore put on the full armor of God, so that when the day of evil comes, you may be able to stand your ground, and after you have done everything, to stand. Stand firm then, with the belt of truth buckled around your waist, with the breastplate of righteousness in place, and with your feet fitted with the readiness that comes from the gospel of peace. In addition to all this, take up the shield of faith, with which you can extinguish all the flaming arrows of the evil one. Take the helmet of salvation and the sword of the Spirit, which is the word of God.
>
> And pray in the Spirit on all occasions with all kinds of prayers and requests. With this in mind, be alert and always keep on praying for all the Lord's people.
> *Ephesians 6:10-18*

Even though we are weak, our Lord has provided us with the armor and weapons to fight the Evil One, no matter how deep the evil goes. My main advice to anybody who starts to see these things taking place is that we have to recognize that the message of the Bible is true. Yes, we realize there is bad news, so, many ugly things are happening. There is a spiritual cancer, sin, that is rampant and all of us are guilty. I mean the world has a spiritual cancer called sin and rebellion against God.

But always remember, there is the Good News, too. "Everyone who calls on the name of the Lord will be saved." (Romans 10:13) The Bible says it, and it really is that simple. If you truly, in your heart, believe, your change of heart will lead you to the Lord. It's by God's grace. We can't work for grace, the divine favor of the Lord. You cannot earn it.

John 3:16 is probably the most popular verse in the Bible. "For God so loved the world that he gave his one and only Son, that whoever believes in him shall not perish but have eternal life." But so often, we don't delve deeper into the rest of the passage. There it goes on to say, that God did not send his son to condemn the world, but to save the world, but through the actions of men, they are condemned. Men loved the darkness more than the light. Men hide from the light lest their deeds be exposed.

So, the conclusion is simple. Cast your cares on the Lord. We need to be getting ourselves and everyone we know to Christ. We must get men and women to see themselves as lost sinners, and save them so that they also can receive the mercy of the Savior. On him alone can we trust. While the New World Order is something we all need to be aware of, in the long run, we will have the victory in the Lord, Jesus Christ.

# BIBLIOGRAPHY

Baer, Randall N. *Inside the New Age Nightmare.* Rochester, VT: Huntington House, 1989.

Bailey, Alice. *The Unfinished Autobiography.* United Kingdom: Lucis Press Ltd, 1973.

Bailey, Alice. *The Externalisation of the Hierarchy.* United Kingdom: Lucis Press Ltd, 1973.

Bailey, Foster. *Running God's Plan.* New York: Lucis Publishing Co, 1972.

Blavatsky, H. P. The Secret Doctrine: The Synthesis of Science, Religion, and Philosophy, Vol. I — Cosmogenesis. Theosophical University Press, 1999 reprint of 1888 ed.

——. *The Secret Doctrine: The Synthesis of Science, Religion, and Philosophy, Vol. II — Anthropogenesis.* Theosophical University Press, 1999 reprint of 1888 ed.

Brown, Gordon. Speech at the Progressive Governance Conference. February 19, 2010.

Bush, George H. W. Address to the Nation on the Invasion of Iraq. January 16, 1991.

Cooper, William. *Majesty Twelve.* William Cooper, 1997.

——. *Mystery Babylon: Part 37 – Rose Cross College, Part 2.* As transcribed in http://deceivedworld.blogspot. com, October 3, 2010.

Crowley, Aleister. *The Confessions of Aleister Crowley.* New York: Bantam Books, Inc., 1971.

Disraeli, Benjamin. *Conigsby; Or, the New Generation.* Whitefish, MT: Kessinger Publishing Company, 2005 (reprint).

Farage, Nigel. European Parliament, Brussels. Debate: European Council and Commission statements - EU 2020. - Follow-up of the informal European Council of 11 February 2010.

Griffin, G. Edward. *The Creature from Jekyll Island: A Second Look at the Federal Reserve.* New York: American Media, 1998.

——. *Transcript of Norman Dodd Interview.* New York: American Media, 1982.

Hall, Manly P. *America's Assignment with Destiny.* United States: Philosophical Research Society Inc., 1989.

——. *An Encyclopedic Outline of Masonic Hermetic Qabbalistic and Rosicrucian Symbolical Philosophy.* United States: Philosophical Research Society, 1988.

——. *The Lost Keys of Freemasonry.* Dover: Dover Publications Inc., 2009.

Hunt, Dave. *A Woman Rides the Beast: The Roman Catholic Church and the Last Days.* Irvine, CA: Harvest House Publishers, 1994.

——, and McMahon, Thomas A. *America: the Sorcerer's New Apprentice.* Irvine, CA: Harvest House Publishers, 1994.

"Interview w/ Christopher Monckton." *Glenn Beck Show*, October 30, 2009.

Jones, Alex. *Dark Secrets: Inside Bohemian Grove.* Austin, TX: Alex Jones' Infowars.com, 2000.

Marx, Karl. *Love Poems of Karl Marx.* San Francisco, CA: City Lights Books, 1977.

Missler, Chuck. *Learn the Bible in 24 Hours.* Nashville, TN: Thomas Nelson Inc, 2002.

Levi, Eliphas. *The History of Magic.* Newburyport, MA: Red Wheel/Weiser, 1999.

Livesey, Roy. *Understanding the New World Order: World Government and World Religion.* Great Britain: New Wine Ministries, 1986.

Michaelson, Johanna. *The Beautiful Side of Evil.* Irvine, CA: Harvest House Publishers, 1982.

*The Occult Digest: A Magazine for Everybody.* Kessinger Publishing, LLC, January 1931.

Pike, Albert. *Morals and Dogma of the Ancient and Accepted Scottish Rite of Freemasonry.* Washington, D.C.: L.H. Jenkins, 1954 (reprint).

Quigley, Carroll. *Tragedy & Hope: A History of the World in Our Time.* G S G & Associates Pub, 1975.

Riefenstahl, Leni and Ruttman, Walter. *Triumph of the Will (Triumph des Willens).* Nuremburg, Germany: Leni Riefenstahl-Produktion, 1934.

Rice, John R. *The King of the Jews.* Murfreesboro, TN: Sword of the Lord, 1955.

Warburg, Paul. Address to the US Senate, February 17, 1950.

Wells, H.G. *The New World Order.* London: Secker and Warburg, 1940.

Wurmbrand, Richard. *Marx & Satan.* Bartlesville, OK: Voice of the Martyrs Publishers, 1990.

CPSIA information can be obtained at www.ICGtesting.com
Printed in the USA
LVOW13s0517250813

349440LV00002B/408/P